# From Farm Girl to Missionary

## The Life of Mary Haskell Rentfro

by
Jean M. Anderson

**TEACH Services, Inc.**
P U B L I S H I N G
www.TEACHServices.com • (800) 367-1844

World rights reserved. This book or any portion thereof may not be copied or reproduced in any form or manner whatever, except as provided by law, without the written permission of the publisher, except by a reviewer who may quote brief passages in a review.

The author assumes full responsibility for the accuracy of all facts and quotations as cited in this book. The opinions expressed in this book are the author's personal views and interpretations, and do not necessarily reflect those of the publisher.

This book is provided with the understanding that the publisher is not engaged in giving spiritual, legal, medical, or other professional advice. If authoritative advice is needed, the reader should seek the counsel of a competent professional.

Copyright © 2019 Jean M. Anderson

Copyright © 2019 TEACH Services, Inc.

ISBN-13: 978-1-4796-1039-6 (Paperback)

ISBN-13: 978-1-4796-1040-2 (ePub)

Library of Congress Control Number: 2019934082

# *Dedication*

To Clint, my gregarious grammarian husband, who worked a myriad of hours reading this manuscript providing me with legitimate criticism and suggestions for which I am so grateful.

—Jean

# *Table of Contents*

**Section I**
   1. Little Mary .................................................... 15
   2. Moving Around ............................................ 18
   3. The Beginning of Abuse ................................ 22
   4. The Abuse Continues ................................... 26
   5. Mary on Her Own .......................................... 28
   6. A New Life .................................................... 32
   7. Facing the Storm .......................................... 36

**Section II**
   8. Doing God's Work ......................................... 42
   9. The Bible Institute ........................................ 45
   10. Back to Canvassing .................................... 48
   11. A Miracle Deliverance ................................ 52
   12. Eggs and More Eggs .................................. 55
   13. A Strange Companion ................................ 60
   14. Working with Blanche ................................ 64
   15. Country Experiences .................................. 66
   16. Trouble for Blanche ................................... 69
   17. A Turkey Adventure ................................... 72
   18. Another Year of Canvassing Completed ..... 75
   19. Together Again ........................................... 78
   20. The Case of the Missing Books ................. 82
   21. Broken Eggs ............................................... 85
   22. A New Direction ......................................... 88
   23. The Mysterious Violets .............................. 92
   24. Goodbye Susan .......................................... 96
   25. Preparing for Graduation and a Wedding ... 103
   26. The Wedding ............................................. 107
   27. Working for the Lord .................................. 111
   28. On Their Way ............................................. 115

**Section III**

- 29. An Arrival Shock . . . . . . . . . . . . . . . . . . . . . . . . . . 122
- 30. Here at Last. . . . . . . . . . . . . . . . . . . . . . . . . . . . . . 127
- 31. Learning How to Live in Lisbon . . . . . . . . . . . . . . 132
- 32. Starving . . . . . . . . . . . . . . . . . . . . . . . . . . . . . . . . 137
- 33. Busy Working for the Lord . . . . . . . . . . . . . . . . . 141
- 34. Working in Carcavellos . . . . . . . . . . . . . . . . . . . . 146
- 35. Back to Lisbon . . . . . . . . . . . . . . . . . . . . . . . . . . 150
- 36. Becoming a Leader. . . . . . . . . . . . . . . . . . . . . . . 153
- 37. New Converts . . . . . . . . . . . . . . . . . . . . . . . . . . . 157
- 38. The Revolution . . . . . . . . . . . . . . . . . . . . . . . . . . 160
- 39. Trying Times . . . . . . . . . . . . . . . . . . . . . . . . . . . 163
- 40. Family Experiences. . . . . . . . . . . . . . . . . . . . . . . 168
- 41. Back Home in Iowa . . . . . . . . . . . . . . . . . . . . . . 173
- 42. Back to Portugal . . . . . . . . . . . . . . . . . . . . . . . . . 178
- 43. Sickness and Loss . . . . . . . . . . . . . . . . . . . . . . . . 182
- 44. Sailing on a Freighter . . . . . . . . . . . . . . . . . . . . . 186
- 45. On to Africa and Beyond. . . . . . . . . . . . . . . . . . . 190
- 46. The End of the Journey . . . . . . . . . . . . . . . . . . . . 194

# *Preface*

It all began in August of 2017 when Brenda Morris, great-granddaughter of Mary Rentfro, invited me to write her great-grandmother's biography. Since I love Adventist history, I accepted her invitation.

She soon supplied me with eleven handwritten notebooks composed by Marian Padgett, Mary's daughter. There are three living grandchildren, and I was able to interview Arloene Goley and Barbara Post. Dwayne Padgett was not available for an interview.

Barbara Post, Curtis's daughter, provided detailed information about the family with photos and other documents. Since she lived near her grandmother when Mary returned to California from Brazil, she grew up with a great love for her.

Arloene Goley, Charles's daughter, and her husband John also provided material they had collected: photos, family tree information, and an excellent timeline of the Rentfros' work in Portugal.

Other help came from Ancestory.com, Adventist archive information, other Internet sites, and those listed in the acknowledgments.

It is my hope that the recital of Mary's life as an early colporteur and as a pioneer missionary woman in partnership with her husband Clarence Rentfro, will be of historical benefit to others.

With the assistance of those listed above, we did our best to verify the names, dates, and places listed in the book. Due to the lack of early denominational records, it was not possible to verify all the names of the church members mentioned here and there in the narrative. So, we depended on the accuracy of Clarence Rentfro's diary entries reported by Marian Padgett in her handwritten notebooks.

The notebooks end mid-sentence just as the Rentfro family was planning to disembark from a ship into the country of Brazil. Not too much information is available about their missionary work in that country. However, I found some in a Portuguese book covering the centennial of Adventist work in Portugal. It appears that their stay in Brazil may have been cut short due to health problems.

# *Acknowledgments*

Arloene Goley, Mary's granddaughter, with whom I had the privilege to interview by phone about her memories of Mary. She and her husband John provided family photos, an excellent timeline, and other helpful documents.

Iowa Conference of Seventh-day Adventists, Carol Sirpless, 1005 Grand Avenue, Des Moines, IA.

Mid-American Union of Seventh-day Adventists, Penney Marshall, Lincoln, NE.

Brenda Morris, Mary's great-granddaughter, who supplied me with the eleven handwritten notebooks and other information.

Marian Padgett, who shared eleven handwritten notebooks and other documents about the life of her parents, Mary and Clarence Rentfro

Barbara Post, Mary's granddaughter, whom I had the privilege to interview by phone about her memories of Mary. She also provided many family photos, copies of documents, and other background information.

Southern Adventist University Reference Library, Collegedale, TN, Pamela Jansen, reference librarian, McKee Library.

*Mary Loizette Haskell Rentfro.*
*Born August 11, 1874.*
*Died April 26, 1972.*

## *Introduction*

The Haskells were pioneers in the midwestern section of our country. Mary's grandfather, Daniel Haskell, was an early settler in Iowa. Although he was born in Canada in 1852, he applied and received land from the government of Tama County in Iowa. Married twice, he and his wives produced ten children, six of whom lived.

One of the living children, Lafayette Haskell, became the father of Mary and her siblings, Marshall, Susan, and Robert. Lafayette outlived his wife, Margaret Stevens Haskell, by six years. They both were members of the Seventh-day Baptist Church. The family moved several times and lived in Carlton Township, Dallas County, Story County, and later Tama County after fourteen years living in Missouri.

According to most accounts, when first meeting Mary, one was struck with her large brown eyes. She tended to look directly at people while listening intently to them. Mary is described as a petite, carefully-groomed woman who used face powder, but no other makeup. A warm, non-judgmental person with great strength of character and fearless courage, she demonstrated a Christ-like manner to others. As a firm believer in Jesus, she looked forward to His second coming. She had a sense of humor and smiled a lot. She was a hard worker and made most of her own clothes all of her life.

Because of abuse at home, Mary and her sister, Susan, left home to become colporteurs. Mary was twenty-two years old when she started selling books for the Seventh-day Adventists.

In 1853 Stephen N. Haskell, a Seventh-day Adventist leader with no relation to Lafayette Haskell, visualized a way to distribute literature. His wife, Mary H. Haskell, organized the Vigilant Missionary Society in South Lancaster, Massachusetts, that met every Wednesday afternoon to do the work of distribution. Seeing its success, Elder Haskell decided to extend this idea to the whole conference, and it eventually became the Tract and Missionary Society with appointed directors in different areas.

In 1882 it became the International Tract Society. The first real salesman, George King, surprised his fellow workers by actually selling Adventist literature for money instead of distributing it free of charge. After that the first field secretary, C. Eldridge, organized and directed the first colporteurs in their work. Later the International Tract Society was taken over by the Book and Bible Houses. So, Mary actually was one of the early colporteurs who pioneered the work in rural America.

Being a colporteur gave Mary experience in working with many different types of people in many different situations. These experiences were excellent preparation for becoming a missionary. During Mary's mission experience, which began in 1904, the Adventist Church organization itself was fairly new, and members were not used to providing financial support for missions since the concept of sending missionaries overseas was new to members.

Mary and her husband Clarence built a firm foundation for the church in a foreign country where there were no Adventists at all. They also accomplished this work with little financial support. You will notice in the story that they moved around a lot. Since they had little or no money to rent halls, they conducted evangelistic efforts and church services in their various homes. After a group became established, they moved to a new home in order to start a new group. Their greatest expense was for the purchase of tracts, although Clarence wrote many of his own and only needed funds to print them.

With great sacrifice of their time, their health, their private home life, and their own finances, they left close to 100 faithful members of the Seventh-day Adventist church in the mission field where they served for thirteen years. This field has now grown to 9,300 baptized members and 12,000 total people attending their 116 churches. The church also supports five schools and four home and day centers.[12*]

---

1  By: Inter-European Division News & *Adventist Review*. President of Portugal Visits Adventist Church in Portugal (March 5, 2018). http://1ref.us/r6 (accessed December 6, 2018)

2  *Statistics as of March 5, 2018

# Section I

*Chapter 1*

# *Little Mary*

Little Mary Haskell stood by the window watching the raindrops splashing on the pane and trailing to the bottom.

"I wish the rain would stop," she murmured to herself.

In just a few minutes, the rain did stop, and the storm clouds faded into the expansive Iowa sky. Mary spied puddles of water in the yard near the road. Instantly, she became alert and excited. "Oh, Mama," she called to her mother in the kitchen. "May I go out and play in the puddles?"

"Yes," replied Mother, "but don't get your dress dirty."

Mary glanced down at her red and white gingham dress as she ran her hands down the fabric her mother had so lovingly sewn for her.

"I'll be careful, Mama," she called as she skipped out of the house, picking up a stick on her way to the edge of the road.

Bending down she began stirring the water and mud in the puddles hoping to make a mud pie. She looked up the small hill near their house to see the small stream of water flowing down the road still filling the puddles. Then, within her gaze appeared a horse and buggy moving down the road toward her. Fascinated with the sight, she stopped stirring the mud, stood up, and stared as the buggy came to a stop right beside her.

A kind voice from the buggy said, "Little girl, would you like to read this book?" Mary saw a lovely lady holding a book in her hand and a little girl sitting beside her. Mary lost her voice, so the lady asked, "Is your mother home?"

Mary regained her voice and said, "Yes, I'll go call her for you."

She ran to the house calling for her mother. Mrs. Haskell heard the voices and came to the door to see Mary running toward her. She and Mary walked out to the buggy to speak to the lady who greeted Mrs. Haskell and introduced herself as Mrs. Payne who lived on a farm about five miles away near Adel, Iowa.

Then, Mrs. Payne asked Mrs. Haskell a very odd question. "Would you allow your children to go to Sabbath School with me when I drive past your home on Saturday morning?"

As Mrs. Haskell paused before she answered, Mary wondered what a Sabbath School was and why was school on Saturday morning. Mary did not know at that time, but when her mother agreed to Mrs. Payne's request, the direction of life for Mary and her sister, Susan, changed because they would eventually become important missionaries for the newly organized Seventh-day Adventist Church.

Mary was born August 11, 1874, and her parents were Lafayette Haskell and Margaret Stevens Haskell. She was an obedient child and felt secure in her loving family. The Haskell family, typical pioneers, learned about the Seventh-day Adventist Church when Mary was about four years old, and the organized church itself was only 15 years old.

The very next Saturday morning all four of the Haskell children were up early and dressed waiting for Mrs. Payne to pick them up for Sabbath School. As they rode along in the buggy, their curiosity burst forth with questions for Mrs. Payne. What is a Sabbath School? How far is it? What will we do there? Would other children be there? How big was Sabbath School? How come it was on Saturday?

Mrs. Payne did her best to respond to the barrage of questioning, but she finally said, "Just keep your eyes on the road, and soon you will see a little white church on the right."

Of course, this brought on another question, "Why is school in a church?"

Mrs. Payne replied, "You'll see soon."

Just then, she pulled the horse and buggy up to the small white church beside the road in Adel. The children jumped out, helped Mrs. Payne out of the buggy, waited while she tied up the horse, and followed her inside. They saw home-made pews, an old organ, and a platform with a pulpit on it. This was not like any school the children had seen before.

Mrs. Payne guided them to a pew near the front, and soon someone announced that Sabbath School would begin with a song. A prayer followed, and the children were divided into a special class with Mrs. Payne as their teacher. There were three small boys, Mrs. Payne's granddaughter, Nora, and the four Haskell children. Their lesson prepared by Professor Bell, an early Seventh-day Adventist educator, taught them all about creation. With eyes full of wonder the Haskell children learned that God placed the stars in the sky, made colorful birds and amazing animals, besides making Adam and Eve.

After a song and prayer, the class dismissed. "Is it time for recess?" asked one of the Haskell children.

"No," replied Mrs. Payne, "but come and sit with me."

The children, follow-the-leader style, marched behind Mrs. Payne to find seating on the left side of the church and listened to a sermon. After the service ended, the pastor invited them to come again next week, and they started on their way home.

When the children arrived home and saw Mother, they all began talking at once. As she sorted out all the details, she acted pleased that they had enjoyed their first Sabbath. After that, she allowed them to go to Sabbath School each week for over a year. Nora became a playmate of Mary when she went to public school.

During the following year, the Adel Seventh-day Adventist Church hosted Elder Hart from the Iowa Conference who conducted an evangelistic series. The Haskell children urged their parents to attend. They did attend a few meetings, but then the family moved.

*Chapter 2*

# *Moving Around*

The family moved away from the area of Adel to Story County and a 300-acre farm with horses, colts, cows, calves, chickens, ducks, pigs, and a dog. This farm required hours of work. The boys worked the fields with their father while the girls helped their mother with cooking, cleaning, sewing, gathering eggs, and other housekeeping chores. With so much to do, there was little time to play, but the children attended public school. They were never kept home to do chores because their parents valued education.

Father Haskell enjoyed spending Sundays with the family and would sometimes take them boating on the nearby Raccoon River. During the winter he often hunted game to supplement the family menu. In the evening Father would tell the children adventure stories while their mother told them Indian stories.

> *In the evening Father would tell the children adventure stories while their mother told them Indian stories.*

Mother Haskell told what happened when her family lived in a fort located on a hill in northern Iowa during one long winter. One day Indians came and camped at the bottom of the hill and prepared for war. As the winter progressed, the Indians began attacking the fort. Food and supplies inside the fort diminished, so they thought of a scheme to get help. They rolled an empty barrel down the hill every day. At first, the Indians would catch the barrels and open them only to find they were empty. Soon they began ignoring the barrels when they rolled down the hill. So, one night a brave young man volunteered to go for help. He dressed in warm clothes, took some food, and climbed into an empty barrel. It rolled down the hill, and the Indians ignored it. After a while when he thought it was safe, he opened the barrel, slipped out in the darkness, and went to get help. He succeeded in reaching another fort, so troops with supplies arrived at the besieged fort. The Indians were driven away, and Mother's family was rescued. The children loved to hear this exciting story over and over again.

While living on the huge farm, the Haskell children did not attend Sabbath School and church anymore, but Father read the family Bible to them sometimes in the evening. The children often talked about their fond memories of Sabbath School.

Soon Father wanted to move again because he heard of wonderful land in Missouri. So, off they went, but life there became a desperate struggle. After several years of trying so hard to make a living, Father's disappointment progressed to depression, and one evening he could not hold back the tears. Mother took charge right away and suggested that they return to Iowa.

They packed up again and returned to Iowa and found land six miles from Nevada, Iowa. One day a man in the area happened to be selling books with questions and answers about Bible topics. When the children returned home from school on that wintery November day, Father announced to them, "A man came to the door selling books today, and I bought one called *Bible Readings for the Home Circle*. I think it will help us as we study the Bible."

"Oh, Papa," said Susan as she clapped her hands. "That's wonderful!"

Mary danced around the room as she declared, "Let's read it now."

"No, we have to do chores first, sweetheart," Father said as he smiled about her excitement. In the evening the family gathered around the fire and read some of the Bible questions and answers.

Other neighbors purchased the same book, and they complained, "This book is all wrong. You should forget what it says." However, the Haskell family kept reading it. The children enjoyed it so much that they couldn't wait until their chores were done, and reading time came. When the subject of the Sabbath came up, the four Haskell children decided for themselves to keep the Sabbath on their own.

To counteract the influence of the book circulating the area, the local Methodist Church began revival meetings by inviting a powerful speaker, Billy Sunday[3]. A former popular baseball outfielder, Sunday converted to evangelical Christianity in the 1880s. Born in poverty in Story County, Iowa, Sunday practiced his fire-and-brimstone style of preaching in the Midwest. He would go on to become one of the most celebrated American evangelists of the 20th century.

At the time Mary and Susan attended the Methodist revival meetings regularly since they did not know of a Sabbath-keeping church. There were numerous calls to come forward and be baptized by sprinkling. Because the girls had read about the true baptism by immersion in *Bible Reading for the Home Circle*, they hesitated to go forward when the calls were made.

"I feel so guilty," confessed Mary to her sister. "I love Jesus and would like to get up and run up front when the call is made."

"I know how you feel," agreed Susan. "People must think we are terrible sinners when we stay seated."

"What do you think we should do?" asked Mary.

"I really want to follow the way the Bible teaches about baptism," stated Susan.

After much discussion the girls decided not to respond to the calls. This resulted in Billy Sunday visiting the Haskell home. He targeted the two girls and told the parents that he never saw two young people so determined against surrendering to the Lord and joining the Methodist Church. The girls did not change their minds. Seemingly unimpressed with Sunday's pressure, the family continued to study their book. By this time Susan was in her late teens while Mary was a young teen.

This was the year 1888, with especially cold, crisp, nose-biting weather. On a Friday morning, Father Haskell tackled the snow and freezing temperatures to travel six miles to Nevada to shop for some needed supplies. While at the store he asked the shopkeeper, "Do you know of any Seventh-day Adventists in the area?"

The shopkeeper gave Father Haskell the name of the local elder of a little church in Nevada, Iowa. When Father returned home, he told the family that he had found a Seventh-day Adventist Church, and he promised to take them all there the next day which was Sabbath. How excited the girls felt when they heard this!

When the Haskell family arrived the next day at the small white church in Nevada, they saw smoke coming out of the chimney. Someone had come early to start the fire. As they climbed the church steps, a man opened the front

---

3   http://1ref.us/r7. Accessed 12/10/18

door and invited them inside. The Haskells found a pew near the center of the church. Other people came in and stopped to greet the family warmly making them feel at home.

Soon a man stepped to the pulpit and announced Sabbath School would begin. The Haskell family enjoyed the study so much that they stayed for church, too. Because they enjoyed the services and their new friends, they decided to come back the next Sabbath.

Although it stayed cold longer that winter, Matthew Larson, a young minister, came to the Nevada Church to hold meetings. Father hooked up the horse to the sleigh, and the family bundled up in fur robes and blankets to keep warm as they rode the six miles to the meetings. At the end of the meetings, twenty-four people decided to be baptized including the four Haskell children. Mother and Father Haskell joined by profession of faith because they had previously belonged to the Baptist church, which baptizes by immersion.

However, after this, things began to slowly change. What started out as a happy, united family soon gave way to something else. Father kept trying to give up tobacco over and over again, but he never succeeded, which caused discouragement. Although he believed the message of the Seventh-day Adventist Church, he felt he could not follow its tenets because he felt like a hypocrite. Mother began feeling the pressure of the farm work and started becoming more and more critical of the various church activities. She also did not feel it necessary to give up pork and other foods. Both parents stopped attending church, but the children continued to attend. Mother, always a loving parent, started being cross with them about their Sabbath-keeping and felt they were getting too involved in the church activities.

The parents decided that the best way to get away from these Adventist teachings was to move again. This time it was to a farm in Tama County, south of Garwin and thirty miles from Nevada.

*Chapter 3*

# The Beginning of Abuse

    As they were preparing for their move, the girls asked Mother if there was a Seventh-day Adventist Church near Garwin. She told them that when they were settled in their new home, they could give up the Seventh-day Adventist Church. Mother Haskell tried her best to make this happen. However, although the girls could not enjoy Sabbath church attendance, it did not stop their Sabbath observance. They did their best to keep the Sabbath at home.

    One day two ministers called at their home. One was Elder C. A. Washburn, and the other was H.M.J. Richards (father of H.M.S. Richards of the Voice of Prophecy) from the Iowa Conference. The men requested help from Father Haskell to haul their tent equipment from the railroad station to a campsite where they would put up a tent for meetings. Father Haskell gladly complied. Mother Haskell acted in such a gracious manner to the pastors and their families. Every time she went to Garwin, she would take home-baked bread, pies, cakes, butter, cream, eggs, milk, greens, and fresh vegetables. No one would ever imagine that she wanted to give up the Adventist faith.

    Because of this encounter, the Haskells began attending evening meetings at the tent. Three local people were baptized, and elders J. C. Clemens and W. H. Brinkerhoff came to follow up the meetings. Sabbath School became available in the rural district school house every week. How excited the Haskell children felt when they realized this!

## Chapter 3  The Beginning of Abuse

However, at harvest time on the farm, a huge problem arose for the Haskells. The owners of the grain threshing machines took turns going from farm to farm assisted by neighbors pitching in to bring in the grain. Most often the threshing was done on Saturdays. So, when the machines and men came by, if the farmer did not accept their help at that time, they lost their turn, and the machines just moved on to another farm. If Father rejected their help and kept the Sabbath, it would make it impossible for the Haskells to get their grain harvested. So he agreed to let the machines come on Saturday.

Besides this, Mother began complaining about this foolish religion and declared that it was time to change back to their old way of living. Now persecution of the children began. On Sabbaths Mother would try to make the children work on the farm. Also, since she never completely accepted the health reform message, she would place coffee and pork on the table at mealtimes. After agreeing to the harvesting of the fields on Saturday, the Sabbath became an unimportant doctrine to the parents. They began working around the house on Sabbath, later in the garden, and finally in the fields with their team of horses.

Then, Mother began finding fault with the girls. She could often persuade the boys to break the Sabbath, but not the girls. Gone was the happiness of childhood when the family did fun things together. No more reading together by the fire in winter, no more boating with Father in the summer, and no other pleasant family activities. Mother determined to break the girls of Adventism.

Susan, who was a young adult now, learned hat-making from another woman and soon opened her own shop in Garwin. However, when she closed her shop on Saturdays, Mother criticized and berated her for doing something so foolish, for how could she make a living doing that?

Mother devised many ways to stop the girls from going to church. One Sabbath she made wash water for scrubbing clothes and called, "Susan. Mary. Come here." When the girls appeared, she ordered, "Start scrubbing these clothes right now."

*"I'm sorry, Mother, but today is the Sabbath, so we can't do the washing."*

Mary shot a concerned look at Susan. Susan spoke, "I'm sorry, Mother, but today is the Sabbath, so we can't do the washing."

Mother inhaled deeply, but before she could start ranting, Mary tried to placate her, "We'll do the wash tomorrow, and besides that, we'll work all day doing whatever you want."

This offer did not please Mother, so she began yelling at the girls and berating them. Susan reached over and grabbed Mary's hand, and they quickly and quietly left the house. They headed out toward the fields to find a tree with some pleasant shade. As they sat under it, they recited Bible memory verses and sang hymns till sunset. When they returned to the house, all appeared to be calm.

However, the following Friday, Mother threw Susan and Mary's freshly washed and ironed Sabbath clothes outside on the ground, so they would have to be washed and ironed again in order to be worn.

Since Mother perceived she was winning and getting her way, she decided to keep the girls from studying the Bible. She commanded them to stop reading the Bible because they didn't have time to read. Other times if she saw either of them reading the Bible, she would snatch it away and tear out pages. She complained that they were always looking up those texts about Adventists.

The girls still attended Sabbath School about five miles away by driving the horse and buggy every week. Soon Mother put a stop to that. However, the Lord worked on the heart of a woman named Mrs. Mohr. When she heard that the girls could not attend church anymore, her heart filled with compassion for them. She said to her husband, "I feel we should do something for those girls who love Jesus."

"What do you have in mind, dear?" her husband questioned.

"I think we should move to Garwin to help the girls," she declared. More than a little shocked at the suggestion, Mr. Mohr just stroked his beard. However, he also felt the pull of the Holy Spirit to help the girls. After much planning, packing, and hassle, they actually did move from their distant farm to Garwin.

After getting settled, the Mohrs offered the girls a ride to church every Sabbath. Joyfully, the grateful sisters thanked the Mohrs for their help. The first Sabbath they picked up the girls, Mother met them when they returned home from church and asked them to stop coming. The Mohrs complied, and now they could do nothing but pray for the girls.

Mother felt satisfied that she had taken care of the problem of church attendance. However, the next Sabbath Susan and Mary walked the five miles to church. Susan and Mary never complained, but just prayed for help from the Lord.

Father and the boys saw what the girls were going through. Marshall, the oldest, moved out and found a job with a Seventh-day Baptist. Later, he joined the Garwin Seventh-day Adventist Church. Robert, being the youngest, decided that he had to live with his parents, so he went along with them. Father did not interfere with Mother and the girls.

*Chapter 4*
# *The Abuse Continues*

Susan continued with her hat store business in Garwin during the summer months, but due to the harsh winters, she closed her shop until better weather arrived. In the meantime Mary attended school with the hope of becoming a teacher. During the cold weather, she often stayed with the Haits in Toledo to be closer to school.

One bitterly cold, snowy Friday, Mary needed to go home. So finding a ride to Garwin, she plodded the rest of the way through the snowdrifts and snow banks with difficulty due to the low visibility. When she arrived home, she walked in and peeled off her layers of warm clothing. She looked for Susan, but could not find her. "Where's Susan?" she inquired of Mother.

"She got mad and left home," casually announced Mother.

"On such a stormy day?" exclaimed Mary. "Where did she go?"

"Well, she just cut across the pasture and went south out on the road," answered Mother.

Susan did not come back the next day or the next. Broken-hearted without her sister, Mary prayed fervently every day for her. Where did she go? Did she get lost in the storm? Is she still alive? Questions swirled around in her brain like oil poured on water. Nearly two weeks passed before the family heard from Susan.

At that time an elderly farmer, Mr. Welton who lived eight miles away, knocked at the kitchen door. He said, "I came to tell you how grateful we are to Susan because the day she came to our house, my wife was very sick with pneumonia. Susan was like an angel that appeared when we needed help. I came to pick up some of her clothes." Susan remained with his family for six weeks and did not communicate with her family.

When Susan did return home, she told Mary what had really happened. The day she left Mother had given her a terrible beating and ordered her to leave and never come back. When she ran out of the house, she had no idea where to go. The cold wind whined around her ears, and the snow pelted her face. She kept walking for miles and miles crying as she walked, but she finally had to choke back the tears because they were freezing on her cheeks. Just as it grew dark, she glimpsed a farmhouse in the distance. She waded through the deep snow, reached the door, and knocked. The Weltons gasped in surprise to see a young girl out on such a stormy night and gratefully welcomed her into their home.

When Mary heard Susan's story, tears came to her eyes. The girls wondered why they had to suffer persecution from their own mother. Then Mary spoke thoughtfully, "From what we have learned of the life of Jesus, He and His disciples suffered."

Yes," agreed Susan. "Jesus and His disciples gave their lives to give us the gospel. We must be faithful to what we have learned from the Bible."

It was nearing the spring of 1892, and Susan planned to go back to work in her hat store. Mary planned to continue attending the training school for elementary teachers in Toledo, Iowa, with the promise that upon graduation she would be assigned to a school where she could teach.

Mother Haskell, however, was still determined to crush the love of the truth out of the girls. She became so strict and cross with the girls that they feared her. Every so often she suddenly burst out in a rage about "those Adventists and their beliefs." Because of this frightening behavior, Susan decided to write to the Seventh-day Adventist Church in Nevada for help with their situation. Then, she left to care for another sick neighbor leaving Mary at home alone to fend for herself against Mother's wrath.

*Chapter 5*

# *Mary On Her Own*

    Mary was obedient and always willing to help her mother on the farm. Mother Haskell raised chickens to sell. She had several routes in Garwin, Toledo, Montour, and Marshalltown where she sold eggs, butter, and chickens. Because of Mary's love of adventure, she helped her Mother expand her business to turkeys. It happened this way.

    On days when school was not in session, Mary helped her father by herding the cattle out to the road so they could eat grass that grew on the sides of the road. She watched them as they ate, and on some days often walked two or three miles with them, or rode her horse. One time when she was miles from home, she heard a peeping sound beside the road. She searched the area and found a lonely baby turkey tangled in the grass. Untangling its feet, Mary cradled it in her arms and took it home with her. She found a box for it, fed it, lovingly cared for it, and it grew larger every day.

    A neighbor heard about Mary's lone turkey and gave her a dozen turkey eggs to put under one of her setting hens. After a while the eggs hatched, and there were more turkeys. As the turkeys grew, more eggs were laid, set, and hatched, and soon Mary gave her mother a thriving turkey business. For many years after, Mother Haskell nurtured a large flock of turkeys to sell. The family never ate the turkey eggs because they were saved to put under the hens. No incubators were available in those

## Chapter 5  Mary On Her Own

days, so the hens substituted and provided the warmth and care the eggs needed.

Mary always gladly helped her mother with the turkeys. At times, Mary's parents and Robert watched as she took care of sick, weak turkeys and began calling her "Doc." That name stuck with her even in later life. Most of the turkeys needed little care as they matured, but many times Mary rushed to the barn to rescue a turkey from under the cows. Since the turkeys wandered everywhere, they loved to get in the barn and eat the oats and corn that fell to the ground from the cows' mouths in the manger. As they gobbled and gobbled around the farm, they often wandered in the tall grass to catch grasshoppers and bugs.

The turkeys were sly and cunning. They never wanted to lay their eggs in a nest. They sneaked off and hid their eggs in the bushes making it hard for Mary to locate them. Sometimes she would follow a turkey for about two miles sleuthing out of sight until the turkey laid its eggs. Then, she marked the spot with a stick, and after the turkey left, she went to see how many eggs she could find. Sometimes there would be thirteen to fifteen eggs. Like a good detective, she put on her gloves and carefully replaced the turkey eggs with hen eggs, and then she brought the turkey eggs back to the farm for the hens to incubate. It takes three weeks for hen eggs to hatch, but turkey eggs hatch in four weeks. The turkeys could not sit on their own eggs because they would irresponsibly wander off and leave their eggs vulnerable to wolves and coyotes as soon as they hatched.

One afternoon in the early summer Mary sat in the dining room reading when she heard the turkeys having a gobblefest outside. The noise grew louder and louder as they neared the house. Mary closed her book and went to the front door. As she opened the screen door, she saw a large snake slithering up the porch steps. She quickly jerked the door shut, called for Mother, and rang the dinner bell which signaled the men in the fields to come to the house. Since it wasn't time for dinner, they came running bringing a hoe and a hay fork.

"What's wrong?" yelled Father as he and Robert neared the front porch. Slyly, sneaking silently into the nearby currant bushes, the snake hid from view.

"It's a snake," screamed Mary as she pointed to the bushes.

As Father and Robert came closer, it coiled and raised its head to strike. The men called their big dog, Ring, to attack the snake, but the snake was too much for him, and he backed off. So Father and Robert attacked the snake with the hoe and hay fork. After killing the snake, they measured it to find it was sixteen feet long.

As Mary matured into her late teens, she knew that Mother Haskell was really a kind person even though she was often cross with her and her sister. One day when Robert went out to the shed he and Father had built for the cows during the cold winter, he began milking the ones gathered inside. Instead of the usual calm milking time, the cow Robert was milking began snorting and suddenly ran outside. Robert could not figure out why the cow was acting like that. He looked around in the shed thinking an animal might be hiding there frightening the cow. He noticed a mound of straw and gave it a kick. "Ouch!" came a voice from the mound, and out jumped a man. He and Robert stood staring at each other in shock.

Finally Robert broke the silence by shouting, "Just what do you think you are doing in here?"

The man explained to Robert that he was a peddler, and when he had asked around for a place to sleep overnight out of the cold, no one welcomed him inside. Since he had been refused so many times, it got late, and he really needed to find some place to rest. He saw the huge shelter with the cows inside and did not want to disturb the family because it was late, so he piled up some straw in the corner and crawled under it. He knew the warmth from the cows would help him to have a good night's sleep. He said he meant no harm.

So, Robert took him to the house and told his mother what happened. Mother Haskell treated him very kindly by fixing him a warm breakfast and buying some articles that he was selling—needles, thread, and pots. He soon went happily on his way.

Mother Haskell often acted pleasantly to the family during the week, but on Fridays she became cross. When the men went out to the fields on Friday, she would cuss, rage, and accuse Mary of all kinds of bad things. Some days she would rant and rave and even strike Mary when she walked near her with whatever object she had in her hand.

One particular Friday, her brother unexpectedly returned to the house from working in the fields with Father. Robert was a tall, strong young man at this time, and he had observed the strained relationship between Mother and Mary. So, as he came cautiously up the steps, he heard Mother ranting and raving, so he flung open the back door to see Mary trying to help her Mother in the kitchen. Down Mary's face flowed a continual trail of tears, but Robert heard no sobbing. Mary was stifling her sobs for fear of aggravating Mother further, but her tears flowed without stopping. In her heart she could not understand why her Mother could not be kind and loving to her. She tried to do everything her Mother asked her to do.

## Chapter 5  Mary On Her Own

Mother continued to rage right in front of Robert. He stood there listening to her until he could not stand it any longer. Thinking fast, he remembered the Hait family where Mary had stayed while in school. Speaking boldly in a firm tone, he said to Mary, "Go pack your suitcase. I'm taking you to Toledo. I'll go harness the horse to the buggy." With that, he strode out of the house to the barn.

Mary rushed out of the kitchen, up to her room, tossed some clothes into her suitcase, and ran out of the house to meet Robert at the barn. They quickly left home, and Robert delivered her safely to the Hait family to stay for a few days. After several days, Robert and Susan came to take her back to the farm.

*Chapter 6*
# A New Life

As the siblings traveled back home together, Susan told Mary that they were just going home to get their clothes because they were really going to the town of Adel. Susan had made arrangements for them both to sell Seventh-day Adventist books to earn a living. Mr. Knight, a Baptist man whose family befriended the girls in the past, would be coming in the morning with his horse and buggy to take the girls and their things to the railroad station. Mary felt relieved to get away from the abuse, but she also felt sad about moving out of her childhood home.

> *Mary felt relieved to get away from the abuse, but she also felt sad about moving out of her childhood home.*

When Mother Haskell saw the girls packing, she could not stand the thought of her girls leaving, so she called to Mary and suggested they take a walk together. They walked along silently until Mother finally stated, "Susan is determined to leave home, I see. Are you planning to leave, too?"

When Mary, worried and fearful, nodded her head up and down, Mother's voice reached a higher pitch. "You better change your mind and stay with me. I'll buy you nice clothes. We'll give you a good education. That's what you are working for, isn't it? We will see that you get it. Now, won't you give up this nonsense religion?"

## Chapter 6  A New Life

Suddenly, Mary's voice came back strongly, "No, Mother," she answered without hesitation. "I cannot give it up. Not even death can separate me from the love of Jesus and what He means to me."

Like Moses, Mary chose to serve her Master and forsake home, parents, and possible riches and fame. She along with her sister, Susan, had long ago determined to hold onto the truth that they had studied and learned to love.

When Mother saw that her promises and coaxing did not sway Mary, she turned into a raging woman, picked up a nearby stick and holding it high above her head, she hit Mary across the shoulders. Mary ran as fast as she could back to the house where the family gathered. Realizing how frightened Mary was, Father quieted Mother as she came rushing in the door telling her to leave the girls alone.

Darkness came, and the family ate their evening meal, washed the dishes, and cleaned up the kitchen. The girls went upstairs to their bedroom to try to sleep there for the last time. Sleep became impossible though because the girls wondered what the next day would bring. They heard their parents talking below.

Mother was saying, "Why do they want to leave home? They have everything here. If it wasn't for that Adventist religion! Pa, if you hadn't bought that book from the book agent, we wouldn't be in this mess." She raved on and on.

Father tried to quiet her, and he admonished her, "You'll wake up the girls."

"I can't stand it any longer," she yelled. "I'm going upstairs and whip both of them."

Father restrained her by saying firmly, "You have scolded them enough. Leave them alone. Let them sleep."

Mary's heart hurt with grief. She closed her eyes, but she could not sleep. Soon she heard a sob. Susan was crying; then Mary began to cry. Mary suggested to Susan, "Let's kneel by our bed and ask God to give us faith, strength, and peace of mind." As they prayed out loud, they heard footsteps on the stairs. They knew it was Mother. What would she do?

Mother stopped by their bedroom door, and she heard Mary praying for her. This was too much for her, so she slowly descended the stairs. The girls finished praying and crawled back into bed. With peace in their hearts, they fell asleep.

Suddenly Mary awoke with a start. Susan was talking and asking, "Do you see that?"

Mary saw that the room was filled with a bright light. "What is it? Where is it coming from?" wondered Susan.

"Is it from the light downstairs?" asked Mary.

"No, the kerosene is gone," whispered Susan, "besides, it's too bright for that."

"Do you suppose it's an angel sent to guide and comfort us?" suggested Mary.

"I don't know," Susan responded quickly. "Let's see what this is all about." With that, she jumped out of bed, tiptoed to the window and looked out. It was pitch black outside, not even a shining moon. Susan hurried back to bed, snuggling next to Mary. She shook all over, but not because of the chilly night air. "Do you think God allowed us to see the brightness of our guardian angels to show us we're not alone?"

Mary pulled the covers up around her and answered Susan, "Yes, I do. In Psalm 34:7 it says 'the angel of the Lord encamps all around those that fear Him, and delivers them.'"

The light kept on shining steadily, and soon the girls felt a special peace in their hearts, a peace that no one could take from them. They fell fast asleep.

As the girls were dressing the next morning, Susan whispered to Mary, "Mother will never try to pick on us when she hears the story of our guardian angels. When we tell her the story of what happened last night, she will know that God is pleased with us."

While they were doing the breakfast dishes, the girls told Mother about their guardian angels visiting them last night. "You shut up!" snapped Mother. "Don't say anything more about it. That was the moon you saw. Whoever heard of such a thing! Don't go telling that tall tale around."

Becoming more irritated than ever, she did all she could to frustrate the girls that morning. Because the girls were waiting for Mr. Knight's buggy to pull into the yard, they went into the living room quite often to look out the window to see if he was coming. Sometimes they would go to the front door to look out. Since Mother did not know about their plans, they did not want to alert her yet expecting her to get angry.

When they went upstairs to talk, Mary expressed her worry. "We don't own much. We have no money and no mother's love either. What will become of us when we leave home?"

"Never mind," consoled Susan trying to be courageous. "Life never stays the same forever. You know there has to be some good moments coming, surely. We've had bad things for so long that a change must come soon. You remember the text we studied in Matthew 19:29 that says, 'And everyone who has left houses or brothers or sisters or father or mother or wife or children or lands, for My name's sake, shall receive a hundredfold, and inherit everlasting life.' God is with us, so let's be brave for Jesus."

The girls came downstairs to take a look outside again. Mother noticed this and asked, "Why are you looking outside so often, Susan? Are you expecting someone?" Just then Mother glanced out the window and saw a horse and buggy coming down the hill and stopping at their gate. A man jumped out and hurried down the path toward the house. "I wonder what he wants," she commented.

"Robert," called Susan to her brother in the kitchen. "Please come help us with our trunk. Mr. Knight is here to get us."

"What is going on here?" shouted Mother. "Just where do you think you're going?"

Susan spoke up. "Mary and I are going to Adel to find work."

By this time Mother was beside herself. She grabbed onto the trunk that Robert was carrying downstairs toward the front porch, but Robert kept going even though Mother nearly tripped him. Mr. Knight helped Robert place the trunk in the buggy under the seat.

Dark clouds heavy with rain were rising in the northern sky. The day seemed extra dreary to the girls because there was no warmth expressed with hugs or goodbye kisses for them from their mother who followed them outside raving and raging. Father came to the front yard looking so sad. As the girls hugged him goodbye, he told them tearfully, "If things don't work out for you, and you are hungry or need money, you can always come home as long as I'm alive." His sadness told the girls that he really meant, "Oh, why do my darling daughters have to leave home? Will I ever see them again?"

The girls took one last look at their home, waved goodbye, turned and walked down the path through the gate and climbed into the buggy. Mr. Knight stepped up into his place, grabbed the reins and they were off. The family stood there staring with Father wiping tears from his eyes while Robert suddenly stalked off to the barn. Mother started screaming, raising her arms to the sky and shouting, "Oh, please, storm, stop them. Don't let them reach their destination."

*Chapter 7*

# *Facing the Storm*

As Mother prayed to the storm, lightning split the black clouds and flashed across the sky. Rain came down in torrents. Thunder shook the ground. "Oh, now they'll get it good. I hope they get killed in this storm. I'd rather see them dead than be with those Adventists and be deceived by them." Father told her to stop shouting, and come in out of the rain.

The three travelers saw the black clouds and the flashing lightning, too. They heard the loud rumbling thunder. They bowed their heads and prayed for protection from the storm. God answered their prayers because the storm broke and seemed to part leaving the road on which they were driving completely dry. On either side of the road, the rain damaged crops, buildings, and trees as they drove along. All the way to the railroad station the riders drove on dry ground. They felt like the Israelites who crossed the Red Sea on dry land. They knew that God sent the protection to encourage them and renew their faith in the plans He had for them.

When they arrived at the station, the ticket agent was surprised to find it raining all about them, but the buggy was dry. "What a miracle!" he exclaimed. "How could a thing like this happen?" The girls had no explanation. It was indeed a miracle.

Being penniless, the girls had no money to buy tickets. As the train pulled into the station, Mr. Knight put his hand into his pocket and pulled out two tickets to Adel. "Here is a surprise for you," he said with a smile, handing them to the girls.

"Oh, thank you, Brother Knight," exclaimed the girls with tears in their eyes. "How did you know we had no money?" asked Mary.

As he helped them onto the train to find seats, Mr. Knight explained that he understood their situation. He told the girls goodbye and hurried off as the train began to move. Both of the girls were crying. It was all like a dream. As the train picked up speed, they waved to Mr. Knight who was such a kind benefactor.

"Oh, Susan, what about tomorrow?" worried Mary.

"Tomorrow belongs to God," Susan encouraged Mary. "Let's think of how God has helped us so far today."

As the train chugged past the green land parcels of corn, wheat, and other grains of the Midwestern farms, the girls stared out of the window wondering about their future. It was the year 1895, and now they could live a life of religious freedom with no persecution from their mother. They sank back into their seats to rest from the morning's strain. They tried not to worry as the train took them farther and farther from their home, parents, and siblings.

Mary broke the silence to talk to Susan about future plans. Susan took a letter from her purse. "This is a letter from S. A. Hill, a colporteur leader in the Iowa Conference of Seventh-day Adventists. He invited us to sell religious books."

"Oh, Susan," Mary said excitedly, "Would you let me read the letter from Brother Hill?"

Susan handed Mary the letter, and after reading it, the girls discussed the offer. Susan said, "Learning to sell books will be a very nice way to earn a living. It also means we can present God's Word to others."

The two kept talking about what lay ahead, but they wished in their hearts that they could have stayed with their family. Because they both hoped that something would soften their Mother's heart of stone toward them and toward the truth that they loved, they discussed this problem. Then Susan admitted, "Only God can do it. We tried, but failed."

The girls bowed their heads and whispered a prayer for their dear mother, father, and brothers asking God to protect them. It was like a dream for them to be traveling on their own to Adel to begin a new life.

When the train arrived in Adel, they walked out of the station and down the street lined with stores. They enjoyed the familiar sights, such as the red brick schoolhouse where they attended school years ago. Tears came to their eyes as they thought about the secure and loving scenes of their childhood as compared to the hatred and banishment from their home that they now endured.

They hurried on to the little white Seventh-day Adventist church that held so many fond memories of attending Sabbath School there with Mrs. Payne. They walked along until they came to the home of their friend, S. A. Hill who had written the letter to Susan. Although he was not home, his wife gave the girls a warm welcome and directed them to a bedroom where they could rest and wait for him to return.

Since Brother Hill was a thoughtful man, he stopped to pick up the girls' trunk on his way home. When he entered the house, the girls were happy to see him. After the evening meal, they all sat together at the dining table as Brother Hill showed them the books to sell and assigned them a territory where they could work.

The girls looked at the books. *Christ Our Saviour*, by Mrs. E. G. White, was the title of their subscription book. This was the designated book for which they would take orders and pick up the money when they delivered it. There were also two small books they could sell for cash entitled *Matthew 24* and *Making Home Happy*.

> *She carefully tore away the paper lining the bottom of the trunk and found two silver dollars. How long they had been there and where they came from was a mystery to the girls.*

After more discussion the girls retired to their room. They knelt in prayer beside their bed pleading with the Lord to give them strength and wisdom to go forward in His work and provide for them in His care. When they got up from their knees, they decided to unpack their trunk. Mary knelt by the trunk and began taking clothes out, handing them up to Susan to hang in the closet. She came to the last one and handed it up to Susan. Without thinking, she ran her hand over the bottom of the trunk. Suddenly she stopped rubbing as her brow furrowed. She moved her hand more firmly over a certain spot. She called to Susan to kneel down and feel it.

"What could it be?" wondered Susan aloud.

She carefully tore away the paper lining the bottom of the trunk and found two silver dollars. How long they had been there and where they came from was a mystery to the girls. Susan never noticed the lump in the bottom of the trunk before, and she had purchased the trunk several years ago in Garwin from a furniture dealer. She used it to hold trinkets. What a surprise to both of the girls!

## Chapter 7  Facing the Storm    39

"I know," announced Mary. "Our guardian angel put them there the last night we were home. I'm sure that is what happened." Mary held a coin in her hand as she handed the other one to Susan and tearfully prayed and praised God. They were more convinced now that God was with them and would help them.

That evening the girls wrote a letter home telling their family they had arrived safely and were with people of their faith; however, they never received an answer to the letter. They both stayed up late that night studying the books. They marked places in the books that impressed them. The candle in their room burned long into the night as the would-be salesladies poured over their books.

The next morning found them up early ready for their new life's work. They read the books again and put red dots beside important passages. By memorizing these sections, they hoped to repeat them to prospective buyers to encourage and inspire them. As they studied, they realized that everyone should have the opportunity to learn these wonderful truths. God was honoring them by bringing them this task.

# Section II

*Chapter 8*

# Doing God's Work

The following morning after much prayer, and with new strength and determination to succeed, the young ladies started out on their new adventure. They each went to their assigned territory. The two timid young women walked from home to home presenting the books. What they lacked in self-confidence, they made up in sincerity.

Mary kept praying to Jesus for help as she strode up and down the street going from house to house. "Please, dear Jesus, help me to present Your books favorably to my next customer. Help me to remember the fine things written in them, so I can present them in an effective way to the next person I meet."

The time flew by as Mary concentrated on her new work. Soon it was time to meet Susan for lunch. Mary's excitement spilled out when she saw Susan and asked. "How did you do this morning, Susan?'

"I sold several small books and took one subscription," Susan reported. "How did you do?"

Mary gave the summary of her sales, and almost jumping up and down, she declared, "Oh, Susan, God is blessing us, and I think perhaps we will be able to actually make a living." Susan grabbed her hands, and they praised God together.

The money they needed for survival seemed more of a reality now. Besides financial blessings, they expressed delight at the opportunity to influence others to accept salvation. It took them a month to visit all the homes in Adel. They faithfully worked five days a week for eight hours a day.

During the time they stayed with the Hills, they had the privilege of attending a Seventh-day Adventist church for Sabbath School, church services, and other meetings. They also went out to the farm where Mrs. Payne lived, the lady who had first invited them to Sabbath School. What a lovely reunion they had as they visited with her and her family.

When their work in Adel was over, they moved on to Stuart, Iowa. There was no church building in Stuart. The girls found two families who were Seventh-day Adventists, so they organized a Sabbath School. While canvassing the town, they found others who were interested and promptly invited them to Sabbath School.

In Stuart the girls made most of their daily expenses from sales of the small books. After working for about a month there, they started visiting homes in Winterset. When they had covered the town, they returned to Adel and Stuart to deliver the subscription books and collect the money for them. They were able to deliver and collect on each order with no loss of funds.

After this, they returned to Winterset to deliver the books there just before Christmas. They completed the canvassing of their assigned territory as snow drifted deeper and deeper making it difficult to walk and finally forcing them to stop work.

Mary and Susan moved from the Hills' home to live with Elder and Mrs. Charles Stevens. Elder Stevens was treasurer of the Iowa Conference. The Haskell girls gave him their tithe and offerings which he credited to the church in Nevada, Iowa, since they were still members there.

Mary and Susan had no warm winter clothes, and their summer clothing had become thin and worn during the months they worked from July to December of 1895. They had no money to buy winter clothing because they were saving for their education. When their canvassing stopped, Mrs. Stevens found a few jobs for them in the area before Christmas, and with those funds, they were able to purchase a few warm clothes.

Susan bought some extra material and made them both hats. Mrs. Stevens liked them so much that she brought out some of her old hats to be restyled by Susan. When the ladies of the Winterset Adventist Church saw the hats, they brought over some of their old hats to be restyled. Elder Stevens decided this was getting to be too much work for Susan and Mary for they had their own sewing to do, so he put an end to their hat business.

Mrs. Stevens was a good mother whose bright ideas entertained children. The Stevens had a large house which was always full of boys and girls from the church. They also had three growing boys and a little girl of their own. One of their sons in later years went as a missionary to South America.

When Christmas came, the Stevens put up a Christmas tree decorated with popcorn strings, bright red apples, and nuts. Mrs. Stevens planned a Christmas party for the children, and she needed a Santa, so she dressed Susan up with a long fur coat and cap. She managed to find a sleigh drawn by one horse with sleigh bells and had Susan drive it up from the barn. Soon the children heard jingling bells, and they all came running out to the door. They watched to see "Santa" jump down from the sled with a big box of presents to place under the tree. Susan had a hard time emitting a hearty "Ho, ho, ho," so she left quickly, and soon the real Susan came in and acted so surprised to see such a happy gathering.

The happy times soon ended, for the girls had to get busy and pack their things into the trunk and some new suitcases. A couple of days later found Susan and Mary at the railroad station headed to Des Moines to attend the Bible Institute for required training. Elder Stevens explained to the girls that at the Institute they would participate in classes for several months. They would learn many things, including proper speech, how to approach people, different kinds of presentations, how to diffuse difficult situations and many spiritual lessons. All this instruction would prepare them for canvassing and for life.

*Chapter 9*
# *The Bible Institute*

Anticipating these new experiences and studying the Bible with other seasoned workers at the Institute resulted in some anxious moments, but as soon as they arrived in Des Moines, Mary announced, "Let's go find Jessie Boseworth and thank her for the wonderful letters she sent us."

The girls had sent their canvassing reports every week to the Book and Bible House office where Jessie worked. Jessie had written such encouraging and cheerful letters to the girls that Mary wanted to meet this lovely person.

What a beautiful picture Mary had formed of Jessie. She could only compare her to an angel in beauty and goodness. They went into the office waiting room, asked to see Jessie and eagerly watched for her to come out to see them. When she entered the room, she did not fit Mary's mental picture of her, but she extended her hand to Mary and kissed the girls on the cheeks. She greeted them in a low, sweet voice, and the girls enjoyed their visit with her. When they left, they commented on her inner beauty, which is the most important beauty of all.

Jessie and Mary met again later when Mary was nursing at the Des Moines Sanitarium. Jessie had become sick and very thin. Mary was assigned to be her special nurse, and one day as they talked, Mary asked Jessie, "Would you like to know what I thought of you when I received your letters when I was out canvassing?"

"Oh, Mary, do tell me what you thought about that because no one has mentioned a single letter I have written," Jessie answered eagerly.

"I had you pictured as the most beautiful person in the world, Jessie, for where could such kind, cheerful words come from other than someone very beautiful," Mary explained.

"Oh, no! I'm not beautiful," exclaimed Jessie.

"Yes, you are, Jessie. Your beauty is all from the inside. Jesus brought it forth to cheer and heal our sad hearts."

Jessie Boseworth died later that summer, but angels mark her grave.

Mary remembered another encouraging letter that she and Susan had received while canvassing. The letter was from Elder O. A. Olsen, an Iowa pastor. They received that letter when they were at Adel, and it was the first letter they received. Mary kept that letter for a long time. The one thing she remembered was his quote from Psalm 27:10, "When my father and my mother forsake me, then the Lord will take me up." (KJV) When she thought of this, tears came to her eyes and flowed easily down her cheeks. She remembered how this idea sustained and comforted them when they left home.

Mary also wanted to meet other canvassers who were selling larger books like *The Great Controversy* and *Bible Readings for the Home Circle* along with *The Two Republics* by A. T. Jones of Battle Creek, Michigan. How the girls admired the workers who were so successful in selling these books.

The Bible Institute consisted of a large two-story house in Des Moines across the street from the capitol rented by the Iowa field secretary to house the Iowa canvassers. The house was divided by a large hall and a stairway. The girls' dormitory was upstairs on one side with the men's dorm downstairs below it. On the other side, a large dining room and kitchen occupied the space. Mary and Susan roomed together, and from their window, Mary could see the large golden dome of the Iowa capitol building. It made her dream about the New Jerusalem and what it may be like.

The canvassers did all the work there by assignment, like cooking, dishwashing, cleaning, and laundry. Everything was well planned and went off like clockwork. When the bell rang, off the students went to their tasks. They had Bible study every day and studied the books they were going to sell. The older canvassers taught the new ones ways that worked with customers as well as how to secure orders for the books. The girls enjoyed their time at the Institute free from stress and felt thankful for the opportunity to learn more about canvassing.

## Chapter 9  The Bible Institute

However, as the year of 1896 began, the canvassers knew the time for separation would soon come because in March the cold weather would abate. So, then they could walk the streets of the towns again trusting in Jesus to be with them as they worked for Him.

Susan and Mary had worked together for six months before they came to the Institute. The field secretary told the girls how proud he was of their wonderful sales records. Then, he continued, "Some of the other leaders and I have been talking about your wonderful work, and we have decided to ask you two sisters to break up your partnership. We want you each to work with someone who is just beginning in the colporteur work. In other words, we want you to do some training for us."

*"Some of the other leaders and I have been talking about your wonderful work, and we have decided to ask you two sisters to break up your partnership."*

Susan and Mary gazed in surprise at each other. At the first thought of separation, their minds said, "Oh, no!" Then they remembered how frightened they had been when they first started canvassing. Perhaps by sharing their experiences with someone else, that person would feel more comfortable canvassing. They decided to sacrifice their own comfort to help others. So, their companions were chosen, and the territory assigned. It was hard for Susan and Mary to part, but they did so for Jesus.

## Chapter 10

# Back to Canvassing

Mary's new companion was Anne Olsen, and Susan's was Lula French. The group left Des Moines on the Rock Island Railroad.

Mary and Anne started working in Colfax. Book sales were new to Anne, but she soon adjusted to the work with fairly good success. Soon the two moved on to Grinnell. It was in Grinnell that they found a small Adventist church on the south edge of town and the first Adventists since they left Des Moines. They stayed with Mr. and Mrs. Peter Baker in their large house with a wonderful oak tree in the front yard. The Bakers had a large barn with cows, horses, and chickens, and a farm hand to help them with the work.

Anne was getting into the swing of sales work, but one day when Mary came home to the Bakers, she found Anne packing to go back home. Her brother George was working not far from Grinnell. He had a horse and buggy, so she could ride with him all the way to Boone.

Mary pleaded with Anne, "Please don't go now. There is so much work to do, and you are doing so nicely."

But Anne's mind was made up. "My parents want me to come home and help them on the farm." So, that was that.

After Anne left, Mary felt sad and lonely, but Mrs. Baker was like a dear mother to her. When Mary left Grinnell, she often wrote to Mrs. Baker to let her know where she was and how she was doing. After Grinnell, Mary went on to Brooklyn by train. There she found three families who met at Mrs. Johnson's home for Sabbath School and other meetings. Mary received a warm welcome from the group. She began teaching a Sabbath School class and giving Bible studies during prayer meetings. The love expressed by this group and their earnest prayers for her success gave her courage to keep spreading the message of Christ's love.

Next Mary went back and delivered her books at Grinnell and Brooklyn. She also delivered Anne Olsen's books and sent her the money for her share. She paid the Book and Bible House for the books they had received and sold. By this time she was ready to go to Marengo to work.

She found one Seventh-day Adventist in Marengo, a Mrs. Hamilton who had been to Battle Creek, Michigan, for treatment of cancer at the Sanitarium there. Mrs. Hamilton had come home with the news that her cancer was incurable. She bravely faced this diagnosis, and she asked Mary if she would consider staying at her house while she worked in Marengo. Mary did so and encouraged Mrs. Hamilton to seek counsel about what to do with her home and possessions. She lived eight more months.

As Mary walked about Marengo, she saw no Adventist church, but she saw a large convent and school with crosses on all the buildings. She felt attracted to those buildings with high gates surrounding them and wondered if the people inside felt like prisoners. Someday she dreamed of becoming a missionary to foreign countries where these churches were plentiful.

One day she met a woman whose friend was a nun. The woman loved the truth-filled books and purchased one for the nun. Later Mary saw the woman and heard that the nun's book had been confiscated and burned. She bought another book from Mary and assured her that the nun would find a much better hiding place for this book.

Mary found a place to stay with Mr. and Mrs. Hoen who lived at the edge of the city, which meant that Mary had to do a great deal of walking to get to her canvassing territory, but she was glad to find warm shelter and kind friends there.

The Adventists in Marengo met at the home of Mrs. Wilson. Her house filled with people every Sabbath crowding into the large parlor, kitchen, and dining room. This group had plenty of help with Drs. R. H. Habernicht and B. E. Fullmen, both ordained ministers who were taking courses at the Marengo Medical University located there. Both wives of the men were talented musicians.

Mary received the task of teaching the children of the group. Previous teachers told her that as soon as they started the class that one student after another became thirsty, jumped up, took the dipper to the pump outside, raised the squeaky handle and pumped up and down till the water came out. This kept up until all sixteen of them had a drink. By then the allotted time for class ran out with no time left for the lesson.

As Mary observed this activity, she asked, "Is that all they do?'

One of the mothers answered in the affirmative. So, Mary developed a plan. Before class she asked one of the children to fill the pail at the pump and return to the room. She then gave each child the opportunity to take a drink. Next, she began teaching the lesson by using pictures from her canvassing books. She showed them the picture of Jesus as he sat at Jacob's well just as thirsty as themselves. She told the children, "When a Samaritan woman came to draw water from the well, Jesus asked her for a drink. Then He told her that she could have living water so she would never thirst again. Now, let us bow our heads and ask Jesus to give us living water, so we won't have to drink during class time."

The children agreed that this would be a good idea. She also asked them to pick up the chairs quietly when the bell rang and go to the place reserved for them to listen to the sermon. The children responded respectfully, and the adults were amazed at Mary's skill with managing them.

The Hoens had a son and daughter who were interested in helping Mary canvass Iowa City. They studied the books and went with Mary a few times to learn the method of approaching people for a sale. They quickly learned how to take orders, and by working long hours and prayerfully approaching each home, success followed. As Mary worked, she noticed without exception how the majority of people needed and wanted to know a living Saviour. The large number of orders for the book *Christ Our Saviour* showed how they longed for something they did not possess.

One day in particular, December 15, 1896, would not be forgotten because Mary recorded its happenings in her diary. When Mr. Hoen came in from doing his outside chores, he warned, "The snow is deep. It's still snowing, and it's bitterly cold."

The group ate breakfast, then had worship, something they never neglected. Then, the three canvassers prepared for their day's work. The Hoens' daughter opened the door just to peek out. "I'm not going out in this storm," she announced.

So, the son and Mary started out, but after walking a short distance, he, too, told Mary he was going back home. Mary told him that it was all right, but she was going to press on.

She plodded through the deep snow until she reached the street where her day's work began. On this stormy day, Mary found most people at home sitting by their warm stoves. She worked all day, one house after another. The friendly people would exclaim when she knocked on their doors, "Come in and get warm. You look frozen."

The words "come in" were just the words Mary wanted to hear. She knew things were going quite well because her book pack was getting lighter as she walked down the snowy streets. As the sun was setting, Mary hurried home because she did not want to be out by herself after dark. When the day ended, Mary counted up her day's work. She had taken 24 orders for *Christ Our Saviour*, and sold $10.00 worth of the small books for cash. She felt so thankful that she had persevered in the bad weather and that God had allowed her to reach so many people.

*Chapter 11*
# *A Miracle Deliverance*

On December 22 Mary had a memorable encounter. It was cold, and snow fell as Mr. Hoen took Mary to the railroad station in town. She bought a ticket to Marengo to deliver the book orders she had taken there. As she boarded the train, she noticed a man who appeared to be a salesman sitting at the back of the car. This was a passenger train, and several passengers besides Mary were seated. The man began talking to a young lady, but she soon departed at a small station near Marengo.

It was early in the morning, about nine o'clock, when the train arrived at Marengo, which gave Mary plenty of time to deliver the books and catch the four o'clock train back to Grinnell early in the evening. However, when she went to the station that evening, she found that a storm had caused an accident delaying the train with no one knowing its arrival time.

Mary soon heard that a freight train with a caboose which could provide seating for passengers would be traveling as far as Grinnell, so she bought a ticket. The bad weather continued with snow and sleet swirling down making the railroad tracks icy slowing down the arrival of the train. It finally pulled into the station, so Mary entered the caboose and looked for a seat. In the very back, she noticed the same man she had seen on the previous train. She remembered how he seemed overly friendly with young ladies. As before, he began conversing with a young girl seated near him.

## Chapter 11  A Miracle Deliverance     53

That passenger exited just a few miles down the track out of Marengo. Soon other passengers exited at various stops leaving Mary alone with the strange man in the caboose. The next stop was Brooklyn, then finally Grinnell, her destination. Mary placed her large suitcase and some of the remainder of her books on the seat in front of her. On her lap she held a smaller pack containing the many silver dollars she had collected for the orders she delivered.

Mary wouldn't have worried if the man had stayed in the back of the caboose, but he did not. He came toward her, stopped by her seat and picked up one of her books. Holding it out, he asked, "Can I buy this book?" He held out a ten-dollar bill, but when she did not offer to change his bill, he left the book on top of her large suitcase. Next, he remarked, "Seeing that you have such a load, I will help you off when we get to Grinnell."

He picked up the book again and pretended to read it, but he seemed to be assessing the situation. Possibly he understood that as a young book salesperson, she must have some money with her. He tried to talk to Mary, but she did not respond. Instead, she was pouring out her heart to her Heavenly Father begging for His protection and for her guardian angel to shield her from the evil she felt at this time.

The train neared the Brooklyn station, and Mary prayed for someone to get on at that station. It was 8:30 in the evening when the train pulled into Brooklyn. Mary again prayed so earnestly, "Dear Jesus, please send a person or an angel. I'm the only one left on this train, and I'm afraid of this man." Her prayers continued, and when the train stopped, she saw a tall man slip into the seat to her right. In her heart, she said, "Thank You, Jesus, for hearing and answering my prayer." Just then the man who was bothering her moved to the back of the caboose.

Mary leaned over and spoke to the new passenger. She asked him, "Are you a pastor?" When he nodded in the affirmative, she asked him, "Would you please help me with my suitcases when we arrive at Grinnell? I am afraid of the man in the back of the caboose." The man took in the situation and agreed.

It was a forty-five-minute ride to Grinnell, and the three passengers remained silent. As they neared the station, the man in the back gathered his luggage together. He descended to the platform the minute the train stopped. Then he quickly re-boarded the train and started grabbing Mary's suitcases getting his hands on the small one containing her book money.

The pastor jumped up and grabbed the case, too. The first man pulled and yanked trying to get the case away from the pastor. However, the pastor held on tightly, and they moved toward the exit and out onto the platform. With a final shove, the pastor knocked the man down onto the platform, and carrying the small case, he jumped back into the caboose to help Mary out of the train.

"This did it," he announced as he held up his right fist while holding her small case with his left hand. With his free hand, he grabbed her big suitcase and guided her off the train. Because it was dark and still snowing, he asked her, "Where are you headed?"

"Do you happen to know Mr. and Mrs. Peter Baker?" she inquired.

"Why they are my next-door neighbors," he announced. So, they started walking down the street toward the Bakers' home. He continued talking as they walked along explaining to Mary what happened. He told her that he had been preaching a sermon at the Methodist church in Brooklyn when he heard a voice telling him to go to the station at Brooklyn and go to Grinnell. He continued with his sermon, but then he heard the same instruction. Finally, he told the congregation that he had to leave and catch a train that was due at the Brooklyn station.

> *"You may think this is strange," he said, "but I believe an angel spoke to me."*

"You may think this is strange," he said, "but I believe an angel spoke to me, so I immediately went to the station with no hesitation."

Mary became speechless for a few seconds, then she told him, "I was pleading with God for help at that time because I felt so frightened. You must tell your congregation this story."

Mary had written to tell Mrs. Baker that she would be back on the twenty-second, so Mrs. Baker waited up that night for Mary. When she heard a knock at the door and opened it to see Mary and her neighbor, she exclaimed, "Why, Howard[4*]!"

The pastor acknowledged Mrs. Baker, then he turned to Mary and told her, "I'll never forget this as long as I live."

Mary thanked him for his help as he left, and then entered the house to explain to Mrs. Baker what happened on the train and at the station. As they talked, Mrs. Baker told Mary that she had been praying for her all that day. Mary finally started to relax and realize that she was safe from a terrible nightmare.

---

4 * Unable to verify the Methodist pastor's last name.

*Chapter 12*

# Eggs and More Eggs

Early on the morning of December 28, Susan boarded a train to Grinnell to meet Mary. The sisters had not seen each other since the last of March. What a reunion they had when Susan arrived. The sisters spent the day and most of the night reliving and sharing their experiences during the past months.

All too soon the next morning Mrs. Baker called up the stairway saying, "Breakfast." While they sat at the breakfast table, Mary glanced out the window. Frost covered the panes of glass, but she saw a team of horses hitched to a big sled. The men dressed in long fur coats threw blankets over the horses and came toward the front porch. Something looked familiar to her, and suddenly she exclaimed, "Susan, Father and Robert are here."

They both ran to the door and pulled the two men inside. After emotional greetings, Father told them that he had come to take them home. "Your mother wants to see you," he told them. The girls had not been home for a year, so they excitedly ran to pack their things while Robert and Father put the horses in the big barn for warmth, fed them, and let them rest until around noon. Mrs. Baker fixed a warm breakfast for the men while the girls packed.

Father and Robert soon loaded the sleigh with suitcases and girls and comfortably tucked them in with fur robes and blankets. Then, they were off with the spirited horses pulling their sleigh as they glided along on sparkling snow-packed roads. They arrived home in Garwin before dark, and with some trepidation, the girls entered the house to greet Mother. When Mother acted happy to see them, some of their tenseness lessened.

After Father and Robert took care of the horses and came into the house, Father worried about their dog, Ring. "I wonder what is wrong with Ring. He's circling the house whining." The family discussed this, but no one knew what was wrong with Ring.

The girls helped Mother with kitchen duties, and after a good meal, the family gathered in the living room to visit. Later they said goodnight to each other and retired for the night.

In the morning Susan stepped outside to see Ring. He crept toward her, stopped in front of her, and howled. She didn't understand what was going on, so she went back inside to tell Mary. Ring kept circling the house outside whining trying to get into the house. As the family watched, Robert decided to let Ring inside the back door. Ring crouched down and crawled from the kitchen into the living room where the girls were. He went to Susan, sat up before her, howled loudly, and laid his head at her feet. He went to Mary next and repeated this ritual.

Mary couldn't stand it any longer because she suddenly realized that Ring had missed them while they were gone, and now he was so happy to see them alive and home again. She crouched down beside him, put her arms around his neck, buried her face in his thick fur, and cried, "Ring, we are home, and we love you dear old Ring."

Tears flowed from the eyes of the family members. They remembered that Ring had come into the Haskell home when he was six weeks old, a tiny ball of black fur with a white ring around his neck. He was part shepherd and part Saint Bernard. He had grown to be a large, strong dog capable of caring for and herding the cattle. As a faithful watchdog for the home, he had protected Susan and Mary from strangers many times when they were left home alone. With Ring watching outside, they never felt fear. How they loved him, and now expressed this love by petting him and holding him close.

Mary and Susan spent two weeks at home. Sewing new clothes and spending time with the family kept them busy as the days flew by. Soon it was time to leave for Des Moines to attend another Bible Institute. Friendly goodbyes warmed their hearts as Robert loaded them into the sleigh, grabbed the reins, and drove them off to Marshalltown about sixteen miles away to ride on the Rock Island Railroad taking them directly to Des Moines.

When they arrived, they went to the Book and Bible House to settle their accounts. What a pleasant surprise when they found they had money to their credit. On the girls went to the Institute to meet with their colporteur friends.

After about a week, two handsome young men appeared at the early morning worship hour. They were both Iowa boys. Clarence Rentfro lived on a farm in Sigourney, Iowa, and Andrew Johnson accompanied him. They had been in Chicago helping Dr. Paulson at the Lifeboat Mission, and now they were returning from receiving training in hydrotherapy at the Battle Creek Sanitarium. The young men decided they wanted to join the Iowa canvassers so they could earn a scholarship in order to attend the college in Lincoln, Nebraska, that fall.

A new, highly recommended field secretary, Walter Mansfield, took control of the colporteur group. He had canvassed in Jasper County near Grinnell with the book, *The Great Controversy*. Under his leadership the students busied themselves with their classes, and time passed quickly. As winter fled the country, Elder Mansfield began introducing the colporteurs to their assigned territory. Susan's new companion would be Nellie Shoberg, a young girl from Adel, while Mary's companion became Cora Countryman.

Mary loved Cora who proved to be a good worker and a fine Christian. Elder Mansfield asked Mary and Cora to go over Mary's same territory as last year with a new book called, *The Coming King*. Their small books were *Steps to Christ*, and two books for children called *The Best Stories From the Best Book* and *The Gospel Primer*.

The colporteurs left the Institute to go to work in March 1897. Traveling on the Rock Island Railroad, they arrived in Prairie City, Iowa. They found only one Seventh-day Adventist in town, a Mrs. Pierce, a widow with two grown sons. One was an engineer on the railroad while the other was a druggist in Prairie City. Mary and Cora stayed with Mrs. Pierce as they visited each house in the city. They moved on to the other cities visiting previous customers with the new books until May.

In May the girls were allowed to attend the Des Moines campmeeting, which was located in a big park among stately trees. Mary met up with Susan there, and they enjoyed seeing each other again, but as soon as the meetings ended, they were back at work. After turning in their earnings, Mary and Cora found they had enough money left to buy their tickets to Colfax and to rent a room in a home there.

In Colfax the girls discovered an ongoing strike among the miners in that coal mining town. They knew it would be difficult to persuade families to buy books during a strike. No one was in a book-buying mood, and they heard the same refusal as they went from house to house.

"Our men are on strike, so we have no money now," they told the girls.

Money ran low for the girls, and with only a little food on hand, they tried to make it last as long as they could. They had no idea how long the strike would last. Cora, who was usually happy and cheerful, became sad. Coming up with an idea, Mary said to Cora, "Let's go farther out into the country among the farmers and see if they will buy from us."

So they started walking. They walked and walked for miles leaving their territory far behind. Then, they split up and tried selling books at the farmhouses. When Mary returned at noon to their apartment, she found Cora had returned earlier. Mary saw that she was all smiles and started giggling when Mary came inside. "Cora, what's so funny?" Mary asked.

"Well, we walked so far, and I didn't sell a book. Did you?"

"No, I did not sell a thing."

Since neither completed a sale, things looked so desperate to the girls that all they could do was laugh.

That afternoon Mary told Cora, "Let's go even farther out to the edge of Colfax. Maybe someone will listen to us there."

They said a prayer for help and set out separately on a very long walk. Soon Mary saw a lady walking from her henhouse carrying a basket of eggs back to her farmhouse. When she approached the lady, she invited Mary into the house. It didn't take long before Mary had interested the woman in some books, but she told Mary a similar story, "I don't have any money."

Suddenly, an idea popped into Mary's head. "How about paying in eggs?" she suggested. They made a deal, and Mary took three dozen eggs home with her. The woman told her to come again and get three dozen more.

Mary reached the apartment first, and wanting to surprise Cora, she lifted the covers at the end of the bed and placed the eggs there. She hurried back to her territory and worked until dark. She picked up the other three dozen eggs on the way to their apartment and put them in the same hiding place when Cora entered the apartment.

Cora appeared as happy as ever. Mary became curious and asked her, "Cora, why are you so happy now?

"I'm going to the store after supper," Cora announced.

"Did you strike a gold mine?" Mary inquired.

Cora went to the head of the bed and removed the pillow exposing seven dozen eggs. Then Mary went to the foot of the bed and revealed the six dozen eggs.

## Chapter 12  Eggs and More Eggs

"What are we going to do with thirteen dozen eggs? Why that's 156 eggs!" Cora screamed.

Mary responded, "Let's sit down and think."

Mary came up with an idea. She borrowed a long dress and a sunbonnet from the landlady plus a basket. The girls carefully laid the eggs in the basket and walked to the store carrying the basket between them. Once inside the store, Cora let Mary handle the business. Mary explained to the storekeeper that the strike affected their ability to work and asked him if he could use the eggs.

The storekeeper decided to buy the eggs, and the girls were able to take home needed groceries that kept them from starvation until the strike ended after several weeks. The girls went back to work in the city and sold many books. They moved on to sell in all the towns that Mary worked the year before, and soon December came. The girls delivered their orders, and Cora returned to her home in southern Iowa.

*Chapter 13*

# A Strange Companion

Mary's thoughts often returned to her home in Garwin. During the past year, Mary sent money and little gifts home to her Mother to let her know how much she loved her. Now she wanted to go home for Christmas and thought that the little gifts would help her feel more at ease about being around Mother. Even though Mother was quite reserved the last time, Mary hoped for a restoration of their close relationship. At the last visit, neither Mother nor Mary ever mentioned anything about the previous abuse.

> *During the past year, Mary sent money and little gifts home to her Mother to let her know how much she loved her.*

Mary bought a train ticket to Marshalltown, and Mother and Robert met her as she exited the train. Mother looked happy as they greeted each other. A few days later Susan joined the family, and they all celebrated a happy Christmas together. Both girls had a small number of books left from their sales season, and Father Haskell took note of this. One day he said to the girls, "Let me have your leftover books to see if I can sell them."

The girls willingly gave him their books. Hitching up the sleigh the next day, he went to visit the neighbors. Later that afternoon he came home beaming with success. All the books were gone, and he enjoyed many friendly visits. He felt happy that his neighbors had beautiful books in their homes now. Mary and Susan each gave Father a commission for his book sales. They were happy that the books were sold, but they were happier to know that Father took such interest in spreading the message of truth.

Susan and Mary were now about to embark on their third year in the missionary literature work. They welcomed the rest at home, but they needed to sew new clothes, repair old ones, and get ready to attend another Bible Institute in Des Moines. Soon they were saying goodbyes and riding with Robert to the railroad station in Marshalltown.

Back at the Institute, they began studying and preparing for another year of selling books. The year was 1898, and in March the canvassers separated and scattered over the state of Iowa. Susan received a new canvassing companion named Nettie Brown who was only fifteen years old. Susan was surprised at her ability to sell and her faithfulness because she stayed the whole season with much success.

Mary, however, had a different experience. This year she chose *Desire of the Ages* as her subscription book. The field secretary, Walter Mansfield, asked her to work in Newton, one of the cities she had previously worked with the books *Christ Our Saviour* and *The Coming King.*

Mary's new companion was Marie Larson, a rather timid young lady, who lived on a farm forty miles north of Des Moines. Their first assignment was in Newton. When they arrived, Mary looked up her former landlady, Mrs. Thompson. To her disappointment, there were no rooms to rent there. However, the landlady arranged for a room for them with her daughter who lived near the railroad depot because her husband was an engineer on the Rock Island Railroad. Mary liked the large house with a large barn although there were no horses or cows.

Marie planned to sell small books for children, but she was too shy to go alone from house to house.

"Going up and knocking on doors asking for interviews with strangers is not for me," she admitted.

So Mary went with her for over a week. However, she still didn't have the courage to go alone. Mary tried accompanying her in the morning and encouraging Marie to go by herself in the afternoon or stay in the apartment.

Marie stayed in the apartment for the first couple of days, then one afternoon Mary came home to find Marie gone. Finally, she returned that evening announcing to Mary, "I'm through with canvassing."

"What happened?" Mary gasped.

"I decided that canvassing is not for me. And now, I have a new job," Marie proudly declared.

"Doing what and where?" questioned Mary.

"I'm washing dishes at the hotel here in Newton," smiled Marie as she informed Mary of her new job.

Mary decided not to argue with Marie, so she let the subject drop, but the next day she went over to the hotel to check things out there. She discovered that Marie washed dishes three times a day, and when she was not working, she would sit on the porch and wait for the next meal. When she finished the supper dishes and returned to the apartment, it was usually dark.

Marie was only eighteen years old and very pretty with auburn hair and green eyes. Concerned that something might happen to her, Mary wrote to her parents asking her father to take her back home. Mary could not send her home alone because she would have to change trains, and that would be too much for her and too risky. Marie's father arrived without delay and expressed his gratitude to Mary for watching over his daughter.

Mary was alone now, and it was the last of April. So she diligently put in long hours taking orders for the *Desire of the Ages* with excellent success. Many of her previous customers who enjoyed *Christ Our Saviour* were eager to try the new book with a complete reference to the Bible.

By the middle of May, she finished working in Newton. Then, she received word from the field secretary who promised to send her a new companion named Blanche to work with her. While waiting for Blanche to arrive, Mary delivered all her orders in Newton.

One morning Mary looked out of the front window and saw a horse tied to the hitching post in front of the house. She heard her landlady talking to someone at the door. "Yes, she lives here." Next, she called, "Miss Haskell, someone wants to see you."

"Coming," she called. As Mary prepared to go, she wondered about Blanche. Would her new companion be faithful, friendly, and a diligent worker, or would Mary be disappointed again?

Mary descended the stairs to find Brother Mansfield, the field secretary there. "I brought you a new companion, Mary. Please come outside to meet her."

Mary followed him outside and looked at the horse and buggy, but she did not see any girl in the buggy. However, she could not take her eyes off the small, pretty bay horse with a white star on her forehead and four white feet to match.

"This is Blanche," announced Brother Mansfield.

## Chapter 13  A Strange Companion

Blanche came with a harness, fly net, curry comb, and brush. It was love at first sight. Mary went up to Blanche, put her arms around her neck and said, "Oh, my lovely friend and companion."

Brother Mansfield proceeded to tell Mary a little about Blanche's history. She was given to Mary by the Larsons from northern Iowa. She was nine years old and a playmate for the Larson boys. When the boys were young, they enjoyed racing Blanche, but now they were grown. Their father learned about Mary's faithfulness in staying with the bookwork and decided to send Blanche to help Mary canvass in Jasper County.

Mary was speechless at receiving such an amazing gift. Tears of joy flowed down her cheeks for the kindness shown her. She knew how to handle a horse because of her earlier life on the farm.

Elder Mansfield told her, "She may give you some trouble in the fall because she often gets the 'heaves' and needs to have her feed sprinkled with water to prevent the dust from bothering her." An animal with the heaves is like a person with asthma.

Since Mary stayed at the large house with a large empty barn, Blanche would have a home when they returned on weekends. Mary now planned to canvass in the country and visit the various farms during the week staying nights with the farm families. What a help Blanche would be making travel so much easier for her!

*Chapter 14*

# Working with Blanche

Because Blanche had traveled over 100 miles to live with her, Mary let her rest for a few days. This also gave her time to get acquainted with her new friend.

When Mary started canvassing in the country, she decided to meet the farmers' wives early in the mornings. Sometimes she encountered them getting three or four children ready for school. She often observed the dinner pails lined up on the table and heard their mothers' last instructions such as, "Hurry up, or you'll be late for school." Mary liked to have the children around when she showed her books because they often pleaded, "Please buy this one for me."

Working in the country seemed relaxing because people didn't seem to be in a hurry. This gave Mary a golden opportunity to give a proper canvass and secure an order. This appealed to her desire to be thorough and organized.

After Mary drove Blanche for a few weeks, Blanche began to catch on how Mary stopped at each house. When they turned in at the gate, Blanche headed to the hitching post and stopped. If Mary stayed too long in a house, Blanche whinnied for her to come out. At first Mary thought Blanche whinnied for a drink, but when she later drove her over to the stock tank, she did not always drink. Blanche realized it was go and then stop, and this became part of her day's work.

## Chapter 14  Working with Blanche

When Mary was invited into a farmhouse for lunch, Blanche headed right toward the barn. Mary told the farm boys that her horse was very demanding, but they didn't seem to mind taking the little bay horse in, unhitching her, and giving her a meal of oats and hay sprinkled with water.

As Mary worked through the day, early in the afternoon, she would inquire about a place where she might stay the night. She did not like to work late, so she spent many happy evenings with farm families. Sometimes she milked cows, helped the girls get their share of housework done, or even played games with the children. After working Monday through Friday, she headed home to her apartment with Blanche trotting to the large barn she had all to herself.

Mary often stayed alone during the Sabbath hours because there were no Seventh-day Adventists in Newton. One Adventist family lived about eight miles away on a farm, so Mary drove over to their house to be with them about once a month.

Mary bought a long rope to tie Blanche out to eat grass. Behind the railroad station she found a good pasture, and since Blanche was not fearful of trains, Mary tied her to a pile of railroad ties to graze. One day in June, Blanche ate grass all morning out in the pasture when Mary heard a clap of thunder in the distance. She kept on with her personal work thinking that the storm might not come closer. However, the thunder became louder, and rain poured down. Mary jumped up and ran across the road to get Blanche. The storm picked up strength with the wind blowing branches from trees and rain pounding down on everything.

Mary reached Blanche and stooped down in front of her to untie the rope, but her square knot soaked with rain made it difficult to untie. The storm increased in fury, and Blanche acted frantic. She moved close to Mary with her head right by Mary's hands. "I can't untie the rope, Blanche," Mary cried.

Blanche responded by pushing Mary away from the rope causing her to fall over. Then Blanche pawed the rope with her foot cutting it loose with her sharp hoofs. She ran to the barn with Mary running behind her. Because Blanche was very frightened of thunder and lightning, Mary stayed in the barn with her until the storm passed talking to her and patting her until she stopped shaking.

'Oh, Blanche, I'm so glad we are safe. Jesus helped us make it to the barn." Blanche responded with a snort that sounded like, "Amen!"

*Chapter 15*

# *Country Experiences*

Country book sales work agreed with Mary. She found it easier than city work because she rarely encountered a peddler and only occasionally saw another book salesperson. Usually, the farmer's wife made her own decision about what book to buy, but if needed, Mary would load her and the children into her buggy and drive out to the fields to get her husband's consent.

Every day brought interesting experiences. One early morning she and Blanche were driving along a country road with Blanche looking from left to right as she trotted along. Then she began looking to the left for longer periods of time and suddenly snorted and puffed. Off she ran down the road without stopping at the next house as she usually did. Mary finally calmed her down, but she wondered what had frightened Blanche. Mary looked up and down the road, and she saw a big hollow log on the left side of the road. It had burned out and was black inside. It didn't look that scary to Mary, but it must have frightened Blanche.

Mary turned Blanche around, and they went back about a mile to the farmhouse they passed. She explained to the family why she had raced past. The farmer told Mary he would saw that log up for stove wood because it was too dangerous to have it out there scaring horses.

Mary worked on till noon. As she and Blanche were driving near a schoolhouse, Mary intended to pass it, but Blanche decided differently. She went into the yard and stopped at the hitching post in front of the school. The children playing outside caught sight of Mary, stopped playing, and rushed toward the buggy pummeling Mary with questions. In response to their questions, Mary explained that she was taking orders for books. Some of the children recognized Mary because she had sold books to their mothers. They begged Mary to come inside and show her books to them and the teacher.

Appearing at the schoolroom door, the teacher invited Mary to unhitch her horse, let it graze in the schoolyard, and come in. The boys gave Blanche some water from the school pump. The children offered to share their lunches with Mary, so they all had a fun time. The teacher, who was a young, active girl, taught all eight grades and liked to make her children happy. Mary showed all her books, and the children became so interested that they forgot to go outside to play. After the teacher looked at the books, she decided to take twenty-four *Gospel Primers*.

Shocked Mary asked, "Did you say twenty-four?"

The teacher answered, "Yes, please. I need twelve for my first graders and twelve for a Sunday School class at my church."

After Mary wrote up the order, the boys gladly rounded up Blanche and hitched her to the buggy. Sweet goodbyes from the children made Mary feel so happy that Blanche had decided to make a stop at the schoolhouse.

Mary finished covering the west half of Jasper County and decided to move to Gilman even though there were no Adventist families there.

> *Mary showed all her books, and the children became so interested that they forgot to go outside to play. After the teacher looked at the books, she decided to take twenty-four* **Gospel Primers.**

The Book and Bible House supplied the canvassers with the *Review and Herald,* a magazine Mary enjoyed reading. She especially liked an article in one of them by Ellen G. White that quoted a verse that meant a lot to Mary. "Go ye therefore, and teach all nations, baptizing them in the name of the Father, and of the Son, and of the Holy Ghost: Teaching them to observe all things whatsoever I have commanded you: and, lo, I am with you always, even unto the end of the world" (Matt. 28:19–20, KJV). She also read that colporteurs should make the books available to the people, and the angels will record their work and watch over the homes where the books were sold.

"What encouraging words," thought Mary. "What joy to think that I have a part of bringing the gospel to the world! Jesus is coming soon, and then I will be able to meet these wonderful people in heaven who purchased my books."

As Mary worked in Gilman, she noticed how hot and dry the season had become. On this particular day, the wind changed with a strong breeze blowing. Dark clouds moved across the sky. "Oh, I'd better hurry to make it down the road to the next house," Mary worried. A rolling, boiling mass of black clouds churned to the northeast.

Like a train roaring down the tracks, the storm came upon them. When Mary realized she could not make it to the next house, she pulled Blanche to the side of the road stopping under the shelter of some trees. By then the thunder boomed, and lightning flashed great balls of fire shooting out of the black clouds.

"Oh, no," thought Mary as she remembered Blanche's hatred of storms. One lightning strike seemed so near that Mary trembled.

At the same instant, Blanche jumped and started to run. She ran down the road like the racehorse she used to be. Not trotting or galloping, instead, she stretched out her neck and ran as if she had a race to win. She covered the three-quarters of a mile in seconds. All Mary could do was hang onto the reins and let her run.

When she came near the farmhouse they had recently passed, Blanche dashed into the yard. The farmer and his two sons, after running to the barn from their work in the hayfield, frantically hurried their horses into the barn. One of the boys saw Mary's horse and buggy rushing into the yard and came to the rescue. He guided Blanche into a big shed. Mary stayed with her patting and comforting her until the storm passed.

Then the same boy unhitched Blanche and gave her something to eat. Mary went up to the house where she met his mother who invited her to stay for the night after Mary explained what had happened when she and Blanche tried to find shelter under the trees by the road.

In the morning the boy who helped with Blanche asked Mary if he could ride Blanche to bring the cows up from the pasture. As he rode down the road, he passed the place where Mary stopped yesterday during the storm. He gasped in surprise for the lightning had struck one of the trees. When he reported this to Mary, she realized Blanche's quick action possibly saved them both from death. Mary thanked the Lord for His wonderful protection.

After breakfast the entire family participated in worship conducted by the father who expressed thankfulness for sparing Mary's life. This encouraged Mary to show her books to the family, and they ordered a book and a Bible.

*Chapter 16*
# *Trouble for Blanche*

Mary continued canvassing until the last week in September. It became evident that the dry weather and dust from farmers plowing their fields and the pollens from flowers and weeds beside the roads affected Blanche. Mary remembered Elder Mansfield warning about Blanche's heaves. Blanche's breathing began deteriorating. One of the farmers at her last stop also admonished, "Your little horse is bad off with the heaves. She needs help quickly."

Mary still needed to work during October, November, and December in order to finish her territory. However, she loved Blanche and did not want her to suffer. So, she took the farmer's advice and decided to drive Blanche home to get help from her father and Robert.

On the last day of September, early in the morning, she packed up and started for home with her sick horse. What a distressing anxious trip for Blanche and herself. It was forty miles to reach home, and Blanche's breathing became more labored and difficult as they drove. She began to drip with sweat as she exerted her last ounce of strength to take Mary and herself home.

At last Mary saw her parents' farm come in sight. She prayed that the Lord would keep Blanche alive until she reached home. What a pitiful sight Blanche presented with her head hanging low, her loud and wheezy breathing, and her body lathered in sweat.

They descended the hill and turned into the barnyard. Robert saw her coming, came out and took poor Blanche by the bridle and led her to the hitching post near the house. "Your horse needs help right away," he exclaimed.

Just then Father Haskell came around the corner, took one look at Blanche, and disappeared back into the house to call the veterinarian. He discovered that the vet was away taking care of another sick horse and would not be able to come until the next morning. Father knew Blanche needed help right away, so he called to Robert telling him to remove the harness and cover Blanche with a blanket. Then Father went into the house to seek help from one of his books about horses and their problems. He knew Blanche had a bad case of the heaves, so he prepared to treat her.

First, he heated water to the boiling point and poured it into a tall milk can. He used an old sheet to make a tent over the boiling water and placed it over the nostrils of the horse. He tied it so it would stay in place, and soon Blanche breathed the warm moisturized steam. For hours he kept up this treatment often adding hot water to the milk can. Mother Haskell helped by keeping the fires burning and continually heating water for Father to use in the treatment. As Blanche's breathing became easier, Father gave her a drink of warm water. For some reason this made Blanche give a big sneeze. Something flew out of her mouth just like when humans cough up phlegm.

"Now we can go inside and rest until daylight," proclaimed Father.

Robert, however, went outside to check on Blanche several times that evening to see if she appeared to be comfortable. Mary felt so relieved to know Blanche was feeling better that she suddenly began to notice how tense her body felt. So she retired upstairs to her bedroom and fell right to sleep.

When she woke up the next morning, the sun shone into her bedroom window. She arose and peeked out to the barnyard. There she saw her loving father giving Blanche a breakfast of shredded corn stocks which Blanche relished. She didn't have words to express her gratitude and thanks to her family for the wonderful care they gave Blanche.

Mary descended the stairs dressed for the day and went right out to the barnyard to thank her father and brother. She also told Father, "I think I would like to stay for a few days before returning to my territory." She really wanted to ask Father if she could use his horse that they trained to drive single, but she feared that would be asking too much.

## Chapter 16  Trouble for Blanche  71

To her surprise Father announced, "Mary, your horse won't be well enough to drive back that soon. I'll tell you what I'll do. You take Fly."

Mary threw her arms around Father's neck and cried, "I knew you would help me. I remember, Father, when you promised us girls that if we were ever in need to just come home. You said it would be fine as long as you lived, and here I am. How can I ever thank you enough for all that you've done for me!"

Father hugged Mary, and then she headed back to the house. When she entered, Mother asked her what she planned to do about her work. Mary told her what Father said. Mother looked thoughtful, but she did not raise any objection to Father's offer. Mary noticed Mother's hesitation and told her, "When Blanche gets well, you may drive her. In fact, I'll give her to you for your very own because I am dreaming of some other plans."

"What plans?" Mother queried. Mary responded that she really wouldn't know for sure until she finished her canvassing work. Mother let the subject rest.

Mary spent two pleasant days at home resting up. Robert greased the buggy's wheels and axles besides examining Fly's harness. So, with everything ready Mary left the following morning. On the return trip, she stopped to rest, feed, and water Fly at the same farmhouse on her last stop with Blanche. The family remembered how Blanche suffered, so they felt happy to know that Mary and Blanche arrived home safely in time for her to receive treatment.

Since there were no radios, televisions, cell phones, or daily papers in those days, the country people had no source of news. It was exciting for them to hear Mary's news. The farmer's wife invited Mary to stay for lunch so they could visit.

After lunch Mary went on her way hoping to reach her apartment in Gilman before dark. Arriving on time she took care of Fly and put her securely in the barn.

*Chapter 17*
# A Turkey Adventure

The next day Mary began working her territory again. October was a busy month for farmers because of crop harvesting. When Mary knocked on doors, she found that most of the time the family was not inside but out in the fields working on digging potatoes or other crops. Children worked, too, especially the boys. School attendance was not required, so most often the boys were kept home, but if there were no boys, then the girls stayed home.

At her first stop she found no one there, so Mary decided to drive out in the fields to meet the family because she never liked to pass up a house. She found the family digging potatoes and showed her books to them. She made a sale, so she persevered using this method as she traveled, and soon November arrived.

One November day as Mary drove the country roads selling her books, she stopped at a farmhouse and met a worried farm lady who responded to her knock by saying, "Come in, but please excuse me for a minute. I'm on the phone." As Mary sat at the kitchen table, she listened to the woman explain to her neighbor, "I'm so worried. My large flock of turkeys is sick. Four have died." The woman continued the sad story.

When she hung up, Mary tried to show her the books. However, she told Mary that she couldn't buy a thing because her turkeys were dying, and she would have no money for books. Mary listened as she described what was wrong with her turkeys. Then, she said, "If you tell me what to do for my turkeys, I'll buy a copy of every book you have."

Mary remained silent for a few seconds, and then she related how her mother's turkeys got sick and how she had treated them. The lady seemed very interested in the treatment,* so she begged Mary to stay the night with her and help her save the turkeys.

After silently praying for wisdom, Mary promised to return after visiting more farms. She told the farm wife how to get ready for the treatment, and off she went down the road. As she drove she began to worry if she had promised too much to the poor distressed woman and her large flock of 125 turkeys. What if they all died? Feeling very nervous, Mary pulled Fly to a stop off the road. Getting out of the buggy, she tied Fly to a willow tree and returned to the buggy to meditate about what to do. What kind of a mess had she gotten herself into! If things didn't work out, the farm woman would think she was a fake.

She tried to calm her mind down and prayed for peace for her heart. She remembered Matthew 10:29 when Jesus said that, "…one of them shall not fall on the ground without your Father." Looking at the fields and up to the sky above she thought, "Surely my Father sees the sparrows, and He sees me and the sick turkeys."

Mary untied Fly from the willow, got back into the buggy, and drove down the road to the next house. She discovered that the farm wife who lived there was the person that the previous farm lady had been talking to on the phone about her turkeys. As Mary tied Fly to the hitching post, the lady came out to meet her. She took Mary by the arm and said, "Come, see my turkeys."

Her smaller flock of turkeys were sick, too. Mary told her how to treat them, and the lady ordered *The Desire of the Ages* and two small books. Mary wished her success and turned back toward the first house according to her promise to return.

Mary found everything ready for the treatment. The family ate supper together, and Mary met the three boys, a girl, and the woman's husband. As soon as they finished, the woman said, "Let's get started with the turkeys."

The ladies donned old clothes, the girl slipped off, the husband went to do chores, and the boys eagerly joined the ladies to help with the treatment. The boys caught the turkeys, and the ladies gave them the treatment. Working late into the evening, they finally finished and retired.

Everyone arose early the next morning, and Mary began descending the stairs. Just then the husband came in from doing the chores. The woman asked, "Did you look at the turkeys, John?"

"Yes, they're all dead," he responded. Mary gasped, and the woman groaned. John laughed, "Don't take it so hard. The turkeys are all gobbling." Both Mary and the woman let out a long sigh of relief.

> *The woman asked, "Did you look at the turkeys, John?" "Yes, they're all dead," he responded. Mary gasped, and the woman groaned.*

"Oh, John! Whatever am I going to do with you," the woman said giving him a playful slap on the arm.

After breakfast the lady ordered all the books Mary sold just as she promised. Wishing the lady the best for her turkeys, a very happy Mary went on her way as soon as the boys hitched up Fly to the buggy. Mary worked alone from May to December of that year. She met all kinds of people as she traveled the roads of Iowa stopping at every home and praying for the families she met.

At one home she met a man and wife who communicated with sign language. The husband went to find the children who could speak. The oldest girl interpreted for Mary and the parents, and they ordered *The Desire of the Ages* and some small books for the children. Mary discovered that they were interested in the fourth commandment and the true Sabbath. Mary made an appointment with them to study the Bible on the weekend. Studying with the family with the help of the daughter brought real joy to Mary.

\* In the notebooks no information was given about the treatment for the turkeys. Some hints suggested that it was messy, and it may have consisted of pressing smelly liquid from the loose flesh in the neck under the turkey's head.

*Chapter 18*
# Another Year of Canvassing Completed

The weather began to get very cold toward the end of November, so Mary stopped canvassing. Her books had shipped to Gilman, and she delivered all of them in the next few weeks. Regretfully, Mary left her customers in that area because she knew she probably would never see them again. That night Mary prayed for all these dear people.

She packed all her things, bid her landlady goodbye, and headed for home. Fly seemed to understand where they were going and quickened her pace as they traveled. Before dark, Mary saw the house ahead. As she descended the hill, Fly announced their arrival by giving a loud whinny which caused Robert to run out of the house shouting, "Hurray!! Mary's here! Safe at home at last!"

Mary turned Fly over to Robert, descended the buggy, and walked briskly up onto the porch. Her Mother greeted her silently at the door with tears in her eyes. She placed her arms around Mary and gave her a big kiss and hug without saying a word. This pleased Mary, and she felt so happy to be home again. Finding some mail saved for her, she discovered a letter from Susan that she, too, would be home soon.

Another letter came from a friend of the family who knew about Mary and her colporteur work. One time while visiting the Haskells, he decided to propose to Mary by declaring. "I have land, and you have money. We would make a good marriage."

Feeling shocked, it only took Mary a few seconds to tell him, "I have made up my mind to marry a mission-minded man." That ended the conversation and his so-called courtship at that time. Mary threw the letter away when she recognized the name.

Mary made her reports to the Iowa Book and Bible House and discovered she had enough money to pay all her bills with credit left over. What Mary had been thinking about for the last few months was becoming a nurse. With her leftover money, perhaps her dream could come true. She wondered what Susan would think of her plans.

Soon Susan arrived and received the same warm welcome from Mother Haskell. Both girls enjoyed being home again. Aside from participating in the household duties, the girls sewed and planned to attend another Bible Institute in Des Moines. As the girls visited, they made future plans.

Susan asked, "Mary, do you know what I have on my mind?"

Mary answered, "No, what is it?"

"I'm thinking of China as my future field of work," Susan announced.

Mary did not want to act too surprised as though Susan's idea was impossible, but China was seldom mentioned and appeared only in geography books. So, she said to Susan, "I think that's a wonderful idea. Jesus has told us to go into all the world to give them the gospel, so I'm sure God will help you achieve this dream if it's His will."

Then she added, "I've been thinking that I'd also like to cross the ocean to some foreign country like Spain where I can work for people there. I don't know how this could be possible, but I want to be prepared to answer a call if I were to receive one."

"That's interesting. China versus Spain," Susan mused. "One of us would go east and the other west. That would be the biggest separation of all."

The next morning Robert prepared the sled and horses to take the girls to the train station at Marshalltown to attend their next Bible Institute. Mother and Father Haskell both accompanied the girls to the station. They did not know when they would see the girls again, and they both hugged them closely as they said goodbye. Even Mother Haskell spoke loving words as she said to Mary, "As long as Blanche lives, Mary, I'll have her as a reminder of the Lord's love and protection." This remark made Mary and Susan very happy. Soon the train whisked them off to Des Moines, and the family drove back to the farm.

Susan and Mary had not been at the Institute long when they received word that Robert injured himself by lifting a heavy piece of machinery and suffered severely. The girls sent word for him to come to Des Moines and

## Chapter 18  Another Year of Canvassing Completed

go to the Iowa Sanitarium, which was located only three blocks from the Institute. Soon he arrived, and they helped him get settled at the Sanitarium. He received surgery, and the girls visited him almost every day as he recovered for the next six weeks.

As they visited the Sanitarium regularly, the girls met a number of the nurses caring for Robert. During one of their visits, they met a nursing superintendent. How surprised they were when she told them that the denomination really needed nurse missionaries to go overseas and spread the gospel. This news sparked anew the flame of service deep inside the girls.

They also met Edwin Wilbur, the editor and printer of the Iowa State Bulletin, the Adventist newsletter for the Iowa Conference. He was interested in the Institute, and he was taking the nurses' course. On his days off, he visited the Bible classes with Susan and Mary. Everyone became acquainted with him, and he often led out in the morning worship services.

As soon as the Institute was over, companions for canvassing were chosen and territory assigned. However, just before it was time to head out, a measles outbreak occurred. Both Susan's and Mary's chosen companions caught the measles and received quarantines. This left the girls without companions. The Institute committee met again to find new companions for them and called them in for the news. What a surprise to find that the committee decided the girls should work together for this coming canvassing year of 1899. The girls calmly and graciously accepted the decision. However, when they went to their room, they went wild with joy. They threw their arms around each other and danced around the room laughing and crying. How happy they were to think they would be together again for the rest of the year.

*Chapter 19*

# Together Again

In March the girls boarded the Northwestern Railroad and headed for northern Iowa. The first stop was Waverly, a place they remembered well. The members of the Adventist Church there had given up hope of ever having a worker to lend them a hand or even to encourage them. When Susan and Mary arrived in 1899, they went to the various Adventist homes inviting them to find a place to organize a Sabbath School and hold a weekly prayer meeting. Members gladly helped, and soon plans developed for a regular Sabbath School which continued even after the girls left town.

Dividing the town into two parts, the girls began canvassing with a book called *The Coming King*. After completing Waverly, they moved on to Osage where only one Adventist lady lived. The lady happily greeted the girls and invited them to stay with her while they worked the town.

The lady had a cute dog named Fido with long hair on his chin and whiskers sticking out on both sides of his mouth like a little old man. One afternoon the three women sat on the back porch when Fido came along and sat by Mary. Playfully, Mary took off her glasses and placed them on the dog's face. He looked so amusing as he gazed around the garden and up into the tree. But, suddenly he spied a squirrel. Leaping up and whisking off the porch, he dashed out into the garden wearing Mary's glasses.

Mary ran squealing after Fido crying, "Oh, my glasses!" After a tiresome chase, the glasses slipped off of Fido's face, and Mary retrieved them as she panted along not far behind him. Mary decided from that day on not to put her glasses on an animal again.

When the girls finished canvassing Osage, they returned to Waverly to deliver the books to those who ordered them. It happened to be Friday afternoon when they arrived back in Waverly. When they exited the train, many colorful posters met their eyes. They saw pictures of lions, tigers, monkeys, and clowns plastered all over the station looking down on them. They did not have to stop to read them for they realized that the Barnum circus had come to town.

"Oh, no," moaned Mary, "now, we'll lose the sale of our books. The people will go to the circus and spend all the money they saved to buy the books."

Susan hesitated a moment, then replied with determination. "No, they won't. We'll get ahead of them somehow."

"How?" wondered Mary.

"Well, as soon as the sun sets tomorrow on Sabbath, we'll go out to deliver books as long as we can see. Then, on Monday we will get up early and start delivering books just as soon as it is light enough to catch the people before the parade and show that start on Monday evening. If we work hard, we should not even miss a delivery."

The girls worked as late as possible on Saturday evening after sunset, and early Monday morning they went to work again. At one home Mary knocked at the door very early in the morning, and a voice answered, "Who's there?"

"It's Mary Haskell delivering the books you ordered."

Soon the man opened the bedroom window, received the books, and handed out the money. All day the girls worked very hard, and just before the parade started, the last client received the ordered books. How happy the girls felt because they accomplished their goal with all books delivered and money collected. They celebrated by watching the animal parade, then went home to fall into their beds to rest.

Next, the girls delivered the ordered books in Osage successfully and moved on to Charles City. They arrived early, so they left their baggage at the station and walked up and down the streets to look over the town and to find a place to stay. They saw a large church with a cross on the high steeple, a parsonage for the priest and a large building enclosed with a very high wall looming next to it. An elementary school and high school were also located nearby with crosses on top of them, too. To Mary these buildings predicted they would have a difficult time working in Charles City.

"I think we are going to have to do a lot of praying and work very hard in a place like this," she told Susan who nodded her head in agreement.

They kept walking and searching for a place to stay, for they didn't know anyone in the city. They finally found a sign that said "room for rent," but when they inquired, the answer was that the room was already filled with students who had come to town to attend school there. The girls walked to the edge of town and saw an elderly man and woman working in their large garden.

On a whim Mary suggested, "Let's ask them."

Susan agreed, so they asked the couple if they wanted to rent out a room to them, and the couple thought it was a fine idea. The girls were happy to find such good Christians who belonged to the German Lutheran Church. So, they returned to the depot to have their trunk and large package of books delivered to their new room.

The next day they decided to start canvassing as far from the buildings with the crosses as possible. Each day they prayed for courage to meet the people. They had no difficulty selling their small books for cash and taking orders on the subscription book. They worked their way closer to the buildings with crosses.

After a number of weeks, there was one house they often passed by but did not stop at it. The reason for this is that the blinds seemed to always be closed and the gate padlocked. However, one day as Mary passed the house, she saw the blinds open. It looked as if a lady sat in a rocking chair by the large front room window. The girls noticed her several days in a row as they walked back and forth to and from the areas where they worked.

> *I have prepared a lunch for you both using no meat, for I believe you must be Seventh-day Adventists.*

Susan and Mary usually met for lunch at a specially chosen street corner. One day as Mary passed by the house with the blinds open now, the same lady was out in her garden. She called to Mary and invited her into the house. Mary told her she was waiting for her sister, and the lady replied, "Yes, I see there are two of you. I have prepared a lunch for you both using no meat, for I believe you must be Seventh-day Adventists." Mary's mouth gaped in surprise, but she said nothing.

After Susan arrived and the girls went into the house, the lady introduced herself as Mrs. Blake and explained that she spent several weeks at the Battle Creek Sanitarium in Michigan taking treatments. She learned that Adventists had strict rules about diet and dress.

"When I saw you both dressed so modestly, I assumed you must be Adventists." The woman already possessed several books she had purchased from the publishing house in Michigan. "What books are you selling today?" she asked. The girls showed her *The Coming King*, and she ordered it.

After eating lunch with the woman, the time came to leave, but the woman seemed reluctant to let them go.

She said, "I want to show you something." She led them to her pantry. "Look, I ordered all this food from the Battle Creek Health Food Company. I live here all alone, and surely I can't eat all of it before it becomes stale. If you will accept some of it, I'll be glad to share it with you."

When the girls nodded, she gave them a large bag of granola, graham crackers, and some canned food which she put in a market basket so the girls could carry the food home. They felt so grateful for this unexpected gift and thanked her profusely.

As they prepared to leave, Mrs. Blake said, "Just one more question, please, before you go. Tell me why you are dressed in such a modest fashion."

Susan answered and explained, "It's a style I designed particularly for two reasons. It's easy to keep clean, and it is practical and serviceable for everyday work during early spring and all summer."

The girls wore white blouses and black sateen skirts with white hats trimmed with black ribbon with a large bow on the left side. To hold it on their heads, they fastened it with a large hat pin. In the cold weather, the girls changed their blouses to black sateen blouses with stiff white collars and white cuffs with small black bows at the neck to set off the outfit.

The woman seemed satisfied with the explanation, so the girls took her name and address, thanked her again for the food gifts and told her they would see her on delivery day.

Since they had spent more time than they had planned with the woman, they decided to head back to their room. They walked in silence at first, then Susan said, "This is like manna sent from heaven to the hungry Israelites after they came out of Egypt. We will have healthy food for days."

"Yes," replied Mary. "We had a precious visit and a wonderful gift besides. Let's ask God's blessing on the seed sown and for the food received." So the girls bowed their heads in prayer thanking God for such a marvelous visit.

Chapter 20

# *The Case of the Missing Books*

July arrived, and after supper on the first night, the girls looked over their orders for books and realized the work in Charles City was nearly done except for the place they put off for last. They decided that tomorrow they would go to the large buildings with crosses to see if they could interest anyone there in their books. They did try the following day, but they failed to get into those huge gates to contact the people inside.

So, the next day they began preparations to leave Charles City, to stop at several very small towns, and then reach Mason City by early afternoon the following day. The Book and Bible House sent them the address of the only Seventh-day Adventist member in Mason City, so when they arrived, they went to her home first.

They learned that she taught at the Mason City College and lived in a large house with her husband and no children. He was an engineer on the Northwestern Railroad, and she told them he was very opposed to her keeping the Sabbath. Since he became abusive at times, she felt it even too dangerous to live there herself. She planned to leave and had accepted an invitation to teach at Battle Creek College in Michigan. Because of all of this, she could not invite the girls to stay with her.

The girls understood the situation and began looking for another place to stay. Finally, they found a suitable apartment with a bed, two chairs, a table, clothes closet, and a cookstove. It had everything they needed.

## Chapter 20  The Case of the Missing Books

The canvassers divided the town in half between them. The people were welcoming, and the many students living in the homes about town bought some of their small books. They also received a good number of orders for *The Coming King*. Time passed quickly, and the girls returned to Charles City to deliver their books.

They traveled by train to the city, and when they arrived, Susan suggested, "Since we're early, let's see if our box of books has arrived."

So the girls paid the freight bill and discovered that the box of books had been there for a few days. They hired a dray, which is a wagon drawn by two horses for hauling freight, and asked the driver to bring the box to where they were staying in the city. They went back to their room while the man went to get the box, but he came back saying the box had disappeared.

The girls went back to the freight office with the drayman to question the freight man about the whereabouts of the box. "It must be here because no one can remove freight without paying the bill," he explained to the girls. "I've asked one of the men to keep looking." However, closing time came before the box could be located.

Early the next morning the girls returned, but no trace of the box could be found. This ritual went on for several days with no results. One time the station officer acted irritated saying, "We have too much to do to be bothered about a box of books."

The girls felt frustrated about not being able to pick up their books, so they decided to go on to Waverly where the northern Iowa Sabbath-keepers were conducting a campmeeting. When the girls appeared on the grounds, they met with Elder L. F. Starr, the Iowa Conference president; Walter Mansfield, the field secretary; and Carl Larson, the treasurer of the Iowa Conference. When the girls told the men about the disappearance of their books, the men declared, "We'll all go to Charles City to help locate these books."

The next day the men accompanied the girls to the Charles City station. When they approached the station master and asked for the books, the search began in earnest. They discovered that someone else had the box, and it had to be returned to the station. The girls found evidence of tampering after examining the contents of the box. Since Charles City happened to be a strong Catholic community, Mary suspected that might be the reason their box of truth-filled books had disappeared.

The girls rejoiced to have their books back and thanked the men for persevering in the recovery of the books on their behalf. Because of this problem, the girls were several days behind on their delivery dates, so they had to spend time apologizing and explaining the unfortunate delay. They delivered the book that their friend Mrs. Blake ordered, and they were happy to see her again, for they remembered her kindness of sharing her health foods with them. They told her about the campmeeting being held in Waverly which caused her to tell them that she was convinced that she had found the truth at last. They prayed with her and rejoiced that the Holy Spirit had influenced her.

After completing their deliveries, the girls went on to the campmeeting because they planned to help with the cooking and take a vacation from canvassing for a while. How excited they were to see people at the campmeeting baptized after reading their books. How thrilling to see the actual fruits of their labors!

When campmeeting was over, they returned to Mason City to start canvassing again and soon fell into their daily routine. They were looking forward to Thanksgiving time because Mrs. Pierce invited them to her large farm twenty miles from Mason City. When the day came to leave, Mrs. Pierce sent Carl Rasmussen, a rural canvasser who currently worked for her on her farm, to pick the girls up with a horse and sleigh. They spent a wonderful three days at the farm and met Mrs. Pierce's daughter and husband who both taught at College View in Lincoln, Nebraska.

When they returned to canvassing, the girls found that the sale of their small books had diminished, possibly due to the nearness of Christmas. People wanted to save their money for Christmas presents. They were able to take orders for the big book, but in the past, they used the cash from the small books for their daily expenses of food and rent.

They had some cornmeal and beans which they rationed out to last them until they made all their deliveries. Without much to eat, they worried that perhaps their energy and courage would fail. However, they managed to complete all the deliveries and collect funds for all their orders.

With their trunk already packed, they called the drayman to take it to the train station while they bought their tickets to Garwin and home. Having already written to Robert to tell him when they would arrive, the girls lay back in their seats to enjoy the ride and watch the snow transform the world into a sparkling, white fairyland.

*Chapter 21*
# *Broken Eggs*

Christmas was only a few days away, and when Robert picked the girls up at the station, they were eager to see him and their parents again. They had only a few days to spend at home, so instead of doing their sewing and other tasks, they spent all their time with the family. It was too cold to be outside, but Mary did go out to visit Blanche. She missed her faithful friend, but how pleased she felt to see Blanche with her beautiful sleek coat.

A sleet storm enveloped the area coating the trees and bushes with ice making their branches droop to the ground. Traveling became dangerous with icy roads and trails. However, Father Haskell, who still struggled with a tobacco addiction, desperately needed to get to the store. He asked Mother for three dozen eggs to trade for tobacco. Mother did not want Father to go out in the storm, but she obliged by counting out the eggs and putting them in a basket for him.

Father took the basket, went outside, crossed the road, and started to take a shortcut through the orchard. Robert, Susan, and Mary watched out the window to see how Father was going to make his way over the icy path. He walked along carefully until he slipped on the ice and slid down the hill on the seat of his pants. Holding the basket high above his head, he kept the contents safe. Then he tried to stand up, but he slipped again, and the basket tumbled out of his hands cracking all of the eggs. Now he had no choice but to return to the house with egg yolks dripping off his clothes.

Mother Haskell took the basket from him when he entered to see if she could save any of the eggs. "All broken, not even one egg for an omelet!" she declared.

As she looked at her husband who was a mess, the disappointed look on her face changed to a smile, then a laugh. They both burst out laughing, and Mother went to find Father a clean pair of jeans.

After he cleaned up, Father went outside and cut a branch from an elm tree. He shaved off the bark and chewed on the tender inner bark to help him manage without tobacco. He did not venture out again that day.

Soon the weather cleared up, and it came time for Susan and Mary to go back to the Bible Institute. This time it was to be held at College View in Lincoln, Nebraska, with the opening date of January 2, 1900. The girls asked Robert to take them to Gladbrook, which was only a few miles from Garwin, to catch the train instead of going to Marshalltown farther away.

After traveling on the train all day, the girls arrived in Lincoln about 9:30 p.m. They went directly to the home of their friends, Elder and Mrs. Stevens, who had left Iowa and moved to Nebraska to send their children to college in Lincoln. Mrs. Stevens helped them find a comfortable room with a neighbor, and they loved it when they saw it.

The Haskell girls met two other young ladies, Cora Davis and Phoebe Bosworth, who were looking for a room, too. They asked Susan and Mary if they could room with them. Since the room was large with plenty of furniture, the arrangement worked out fine for all four of them. They enjoyed each other's friendship and had fun sharing chores and walking together to the Institute.

> *Mrs. White had prepared a plan for the churches to sell her book and donate the proceeds to education.*

When opening day arrived at the Bible Institute, a large group assembled in an auditorium there. They were divided into two groups, those who would help some of the churches sell *Christ's Object Lessons* until campmeeting and another group who would study their books and make plans at the Institute. Mrs. White had prepared a plan for the churches to sell her book and donate the proceeds to education. Mary agreed to be assigned to the first group, but Susan did not.

When it came time for Mary to leave to fulfill her contract, she asked Susan, "When will I see you again, Sister?"

"Let's meet in the summer at the Sanitarium when Mrs. White comes to speak. It might be my last opportunity to hear her in person. I've been thinking about the five years I've canvassed and all of the contacts I've made. I did what I could to help people learn about God and His Kingdom. But now I want to become a nurse."

"That's wonderful, Susan. You can still serve God, but in a different way," affirmed Mary. "I'll miss you, but I'll see you in the summer."

With that agreement, Susan left to go to the Iowa Sanitarium in Des Moines. Upon arrival she applied for a job because she looked forward to enrolling in the nurses' course there.

Mary went on to Afton, the first town on her assignment. She roomed with the Philpots as she began selling *Christ's Object Lessons* for their small church company. Mary had three more church companies to work for, and by the first of May, she completed her assignments and turned the money into the conference treasurer along with her tithes and offerings. The treasurer gave credit to each company and person, so Mary completed her business and left for Des Moines to see her sister at the Iowa Sanitarium.

*Chapter 22*
# *A New Direction*

When Mary arrived at the Sanitarium and Susan appeared, Mary's eyes opened wide with surprise. She found Susan looking very dignified in a blue and white striped nurse's uniform with a white cap with frills and a bow on her head. In a moment they were in each other's arms happily hugging and walking off to Susan's room as they visited. Susan explained that she was appointed as assistant matron to help out the matron while her assistant took a medical course at Drake University.

"Why don't you resign from canvassing, Mary?" Susan urged. "You've been tramping over the country, knocking on doors, day after day spreading the gospel. Why don't you take the nurses' course, too, and further your education?"

Mary replied, "Yes, Sis. I have been thinking about the value of nursing to add to my canvassing experience. Do you remember what the family said when I helped take care of the chickens and turkeys? They called me 'Doc' and said I had a gift to make them well. Looks like it may be time to put a period on the canvassing work. Do you know that I placed my name with the missions leader at campmeeting to go to Spain if there is a need?"

"Why that is a surprise," exclaimed Susan. "I, too, placed my name on the list offering my life and services to China."

"That huge separation we discussed once before may come true," Mary observed.

## Chapter 22  A New Direction

About that time Susan remembered she must get back to her duties, so she asked Mary if she wanted to help her. Mary agreed, so Susan suggested Mary put on her white blouse and black skirt. When she arrived in the dining room, Susan assigned Mary to prepare the tables in the dining room by carrying trays of food from the kitchen.

On one of the trips back to the kitchen Mary noticed a tall, handsome young man standing by the sink letting the hot water run until steam came in full force. He was doing something with an object in his hands.

Always curious, Mary walked closer and asked, "Is there something I can do to help you?" The young man turned to Mary who recognized him as a fellow canvasser right away. "Why, Clarence, what are you doing here?" she asked in happy surprise.

Clarence extended his hand to Mary and responded, "How do you do, Miss Haskell? What is the faithful canvasser doing here?"

"That is a past chapter in my life, Clarence." As she started to help him with loosening the two sheets of stamps that were stuck together, Mary said, "I am so glad you identified me as the 'faithful canvasser.' The term doesn't seem to fit now because I am planning to resign from canvassing. I want to start on another chapter in my life. Now, tell me about yourself, Clarence. Why are you here and steaming stamps apart?"

"I received the stamps instead of cash for a book I sold, but I've decided to pay cash for the book and keep these stamps for writing letters," explained Clarence. "You deserve hearing from me after helping with these stamps."

The two young people visited as they worked on the stamps that Clarence received in payment for a book. "Where are you going this year, Clarence?"

"The conference officers have asked me to go with Dr. Fulmen and Dr. Heald in a tent effort to be the tent master, song leader, play my violin and organ, and preach. The effort will last till late fall."

"Oh, my!" breathed Mary. "I see you will have a busy summer. I'll be glad to hear from you if you can find the time."

The young people enjoyed visiting for a few more minutes. A few days later Clarence left the sanitarium for the tent effort.

In the meantime, Susan sat at her desk in the assistant supervisor's office thinking about Mary's desire to go to Spain. She heard footsteps in the hall outside her office and looking up she saw a tall, thin young man dressed in a white shirt and trousers pass her door. "Why that's Edwin Wilbur, the young man with thoughts of going to China," she mused. She started thinking about Edwin.

Edwin was born in New York, but he grew up on a farm in the Dakotas, then later moved to Michigan. He began work in a print shop at Battle Creek where he learned of the Adventist faith and accepted its beliefs. When he told his employer he needed to be off work from sundown Friday until sundown Saturday, he became unemployed. However, he received a call from the Review and Herald printing plant in Battle Creek. It was there that he became impressed with the great need of China. He was called to Des Moines to help with the Iowa Bulletin and became interested in the nurses' course, so he enrolled in classes while continuing to work at printing. Susan recalled meeting him there, and remembered one time he had even asked her if she would like to do mission work in China. Of course, she said yes. All these thoughts flooded Susan's mind, but now she decided she must focus on her office work.

As the days flew by, Mary continued to work in the dining room. She enjoyed the gardens and often picked flowers to decorate the tables. As she and Susan walked around the town, she saw beautiful gardens by various homes. Sometimes the owners would offer her some of their flowers for the dining room. As she viewed so much beauty, she often thanked God for flowers and also for being with her as she roamed the streets and roads of Iowa when she had canvassed. She praised God for keeping her safe and helping her to spread His Word.

In the meantime, at the office of Walter Mansfield, the field secretary of the Iowa Conference, two letters lay on his desk. One previously received from Susan Haskell and now a new one from Mary Haskell. It read as follows:

> Faithfully have I worked the cities going from house to house knocking on doors, meeting people, and scattering the seeds of truth. I now have signed a card at campmeeting pledging my life for Spain as a foreign missionary. Opportunity has opened its doors for me to take the nurses' course at the Sanitarium along with my sister, Susan. How much better my life would be in a foreign land if I could add more training to my life's work. I am sure the Iowa Conference workers will understand my decision. Thank you for the great privilege in serving my Master as a canvasser during these past five years. The experiences will never be forgotten.
>
> Sincerely yours in the Master's service,
>
> Mary Loizette Haskell

## Chapter 22  A New Direction

A few days later two identical letters written to the girls with praises for the faithfulness of the two young ladies and accepting their resignations with regret were personally delivered by Elder Mansfield. They also received congratulations on this milestone on the way to their success as they enrolled in the nursing program at the Sanitarium.

Mary became an official student nurse in June of 1900. Now she also dressed in a white and blue striped uniform with the same type of hat as Susan wore. With a stiff white apron and shoes, she felt very much like a nurse already. Her dreams and goals seemed closer now. As time went on, she became a good nurse, and all her patients loved her.

Clarence wrote to Mary, and their friendship grew. When winter came, Mary made arrangements to meet Clarence and for him to accompany her to her home in Garwin. The Haskell family met them at the station with a sleigh. After a few pleasant days, which included family approval of Clarence, Mary and Clarence hitched up Blanche to the sleigh and went to visit Clarence's family in Sigourney. A big welcome from the large Rentfro family greeted them. Clarence's four brothers and two sisters agreed they did not mind having Mary in the family.

The happy days soon were over, and Mary went back to her classes and work. Clarence returned to his ministerial duties in northern Iowa. The new year of 1900 held much studying and working for Mary and Susan as well as for Clarence and Edwin.

*Chapter 23*

# The Mysterious Violets

Spring finally arrived, and Mary walked outside often to gather the pretty new blossoms. One day as Susan entered the staff dining room, she spied a dainty bunch of violets at her place. "That sister of mine!" mused Susan as she smelled the sweet flowers. Later as she passed Mary in the corridor, she spoke to her saying, "Those violets you gave me this morning were so sweet. Where did you find them?"

"Violets?" Mary responded to her sister in surprise.

"Yes, violets," answered Susan. "You mean you don't remember putting violets at my place this morning?"

> *The mysterious violets appeared several more times that spring with no clues as to who put them by Susan's place.*

Shaking her head, Mary said, "I don't know anything about violets." But Mary smiled broadly as she continued down the hall to attend to her patients.

Susan began wondering just where those violets came from since Mary had denied it. With a puzzled look, she returned to her work. The mysterious violets appeared several more times that spring with no clues as to who put them by Susan's place.

## Chapter 23  The Mysterious Violets

As time went on Edwin continued giving talks in the nearby churches and for the nurses during their worship hour. He showed more and more enthusiasm about going to China. The nurses began discussing how he could not possibly go to China alone. Susan heard their discussion and said very quietly, "Never mind. I'll go with him."

"What was that?" questioned a nurse standing nearby. Susan turned around and left the area not interested in discussing the matter.

Another spring returned, and Mary began gathering flowers again. The mysterious violet bouquets of last year came to Mary's mind. She thought it could be about time for them to appear again at her sister's place. One day Mary spoke to Susan regarding the matter. "Susan, did you ever discover who put those violets at your place in the dining room?"

"I wish I knew," sighed Susan, shaking her head.

Then Mary queried, "Haven't you noticed how Edwin looks at you when China is mentioned by the guest speakers at our worship hour?"

"Alright, little sister, thanks for your interest."

Thus, Susan ended the conversation, and the year 1900 went on filled with lessons and work for the girls. When spring came around again in 1901, Susan again found violets at her place in the dining room. She made up her mind to find the culprit this time although she was too busy right then. The very next day a small vase of violets appeared on her desk. No one asked if she liked violets, and she had no clue who put the violets there.

Time passed, and the spring of 1902 came. Clarence wrote quite often to Mary telling her of his ministerial experiences. They wrote about their dream of going to Spain, and both agreed it would be a wonderful calling.

Susan received no violets this spring, but one day after work she discovered a special letter from Edwin telling her how much he admired her, asking to meet with her, and confessing to being the culprit presenting her with violets. They met the next morning at breakfast and began a courtship. When Clarence came to the Institute to see Mary, Susan and Edwin would picnic together with them on Sabbath afternoons.

A major part of their conversations centered on mission service. Clarence and Mary talked of going to Spain while Susan and Edwin talked of China. Edwin had already sent his picture to the General Conference with his request to go to China. Clarence was already studying Spanish in preparation to go to Spain.

Mary said, "Clarence and I are seriously thinking of Spain. That is the country with many churches with crosses on them and parades with priests carrying crosses and pictures of saints." A frown crossed her brow as she remembered her canvassing experiences trying to reach into the closed gates of the churches with crosses.

Susan and Edwin discussed the needs of the Chinese people and how to spread the gospel in that large land. Then, Mary exclaimed, "Susan, we will be living far apart! We might never see each other again."

"Yes, Sis, but we will be together for eternity in heaven."

Mary responded, "Here are four young people eager to go out among strange speaking people and to sacrifice their lives for the Lord. But, you young fellows know that you can't go alone to those foreign countries." An immediate response came from the young men asking the girls to go with them to which they agreed. How excited they all were as they made a commitment that very day to serve the Lord together.

Later A. G. Daniels, president of the General Conference, and Elder Spicer, secretary, appeared on campus to talk with Edwin and Susan regarding their interest in China.

When they saw the dedication of the two young people, they told them they wanted to send them off from the campmeeting in August. Things happened so fast that Susan went to her room to take time to think things out, such as resigning her position, withdrawing from the nurses' course, packing for home, and preparing for her wedding. While she thought about all this, she suddenly remembered that Mary would soon be coming from work. How could she break this news to her little sister who had been with her through trials, canvassing ordeals, and wonderful opportunities! Perhaps they would never see each other again.

Mary returned a little later and found Susan packing. Susan poured out the day's events to her. Mary responded by throwing her arms around her sister and weeping tears of joy and sorrow. They knew, however, that this must be God's will because it is what they had prayed for so long.

Susan tried to encourage Mary by saying, "Maybe you and Clarence will get to go to Spain just as you both have dreamed."

"As God wishes," Mary answered softly with tears rolling down her cheeks.

The next morning Susan said her goodbyes and headed for home to prepare for her wedding. On July 21, 1902, she and Edwin married at the Haskell home. Her proud father walked her down the aisle, and her mother did all she could to make the wedding a success. Mary could not attend because of her responsibilities at the Sanitarium since she now was the surgical supervisor. However, she attended the August campmeeting to see Susan and Edwin on the stage dedicated to their overseas mission.

## Chapter 23  The Mysterious Violets

The family sat together and beamed as Elder Daniels spoke of the sacrifice of the parents in sending their eldest daughter to the mission field. Mary could see the expression on her mother's face and the tears in her eyes. Mother Haskell wept as she thought back to her harsh words and treatment when she tried to break her daughters of their desire to follow Christ in the Adventist faith.

Mother Haskell's eyes moved across the room to her younger daughter, Mary, who was dressed in her nurse's uniform since she worked at the medical tent. She looked like an angel in white. "How could I have been so cruel to these girls!" she thought. "I must make it up to them."

Elder Daniels spoke and told of the financial problems the General Conference experienced and how they had no funds to send these young people off to China. At that moment Father Haskell took command of the situation by standing and saying, "No daughter of mine is going to swim the Pacific Ocean. They will need funds for their trip and for their expenses in China until conference support can arrive monthly. I sold a team of horses to assist my daughter and her husband. What will you do?" With that he pledged his support and encouraged the people to give all they could until they successfully raised the money needed for Susan and Edwin to go overseas.

*Chapter 24*
# *Goodbye, Susan*

Susan and her husband returned to their tent to pack their belongings, for they would soon head overseas. Mary returned to her duties at the medical tent. After work, she went to her tent and wrote to Clarence explaining the evening's events. She told him how Father and Mother Haskell had a real change of heart. Of course, Father never opposed the Adventist message although he just couldn't give up some of his bad habits. She wrote about the beautiful ceremony as the young couple dedicated themselves to foreign service and how she felt the presence of the Holy Spirit working on the hearts of those who contributed their funds for the missionaries.

"Tomorrow I'll be separated from my sister and her husband. However," she told Clarence, "I know God is with me. I'm determined to finish my nurses' course and work at the Sanitarium to wait for God's call to other service."

The next day Mary packed her things to return to the Sanitarium but decided to delay her return for a few days to spend all the time she could with Susan. There was so much to talk about before Susan left, so the girls talked, and even talked some more as they headed to the train station. The General Conference had purchased train tickets to Seattle for the couple, and from there they would go by ship to China. Some conference workers also came to see the couple off.

## Chapter 24  Goodbye, Susan    97

The two sisters with their arms around each other walked along consoling each other. Susan said, "Sis, be brave. I'll be sure to write to you to tell you all about our trip to China and about the experiences we'll have with the Chinese people. God will watch over you as you stay and finish your nurses' course. You'll be glad for it later."

The group bowed their heads for prayer, and final goodbyes were said. Mary thought to herself, *I must be brave for Susan's sake*.

Both girls had tears in their eyes as the conductor shouted, "All aboard!" Susan and Edwin hurried to board the train as it started. Mary ran along the side of the train trying to say a few more words to her sister, but the train chugged faster as it picked up speed, so she could not keep up. She stopped running, took out her handkerchief, and waved it till the train went out of sight.

Then, she said aloud, "There goes Susan Haskell Wilbur, our pioneer missionary to China. God bless you both as you journey to your westward destination." Mary knew that Susan answered her Master's call.

The Iowa Conference workers consoled Mary telling her to be brave for her sister's sake. One of them said, "Maybe someday your dream will come true, too, and we will be saying goodbye to you."

They all accompanied Mary back to the campmeeting where she gathered up her suitcase and checked out of camp. Boarding the train to Des Moines, she determined to finish the nurses' course. As she sat in her seat, she thought back to the first train ride she and Susan had taken seven years before. So much had happened since that time, and now she rode the train alone with God, her Comforter, Counselor, and Guide.

Soon she heard the conductor's voice from the rear of the coach call out, "Des Moines." Quickly she picked up her suitcase and waited anxiously for the train to stop. As she glanced out through the window, she saw a figure in the distance waiting for the train to enter the station. Finally, the train came to a halt, and Mary hurried out the door and onto the platform. As she descended the steps, there she found Clarence Rentfro waiting for her.

Since Mary had written to him telling him about Susan's departure and when she would return to the Sanitarium, Clarence decided to surprise her. He took a few days off from his evangelistic duties to be with her, to reassure her, and comfort her during this lonely adjustment. She needed someone to talk to, and Clarence proved to be a good listener.

Clarence walked Mary to the Sanitarium and bade her goodnight down in the waiting room. After she prepared for bed, she knelt beside it, rededicated her life anew in service to God, and asked for help to be willing to go wherever God felt she would be needed. She arose, lifted her bedroom window, and slipped into bed. As she closed her eyes, she heard a soft song of a bird in the nearby tree chirping its goodnight lullaby, "Tweet, tweet, I am here, too. You aren't alone." It lulled Mary to sleep for a peaceful night.

The next morning she awoke bright and early to spend time communing with God. When she descended the stairs to go to the dining room for breakfast, she found Clarence waiting for her. They sat at the same table where Susan and Edwin used to sit as they discussed their plans of going to China. Now, she and Clarence talked about Spain!

"Just think! It could have been you going to Spain instead of Wilbur going to China," she commented to Clarence as they ate breakfast. "I just couldn't bear to see my sister leave me," she added with tears streaming down her face as she remembered the farewell. "This is the same place where they dedicated their lives to China," she continued.

"Let's do the same for Spain," Clarence suggested. "Maybe someday the General Conference will be calling us for foreign service to a needy field. The fields are many, and the laborers are few. There isn't much money in the general treasury yet for missionaries. That's why your father made that appeal to stir the hearts of the people of Iowa who attended the campmeeting."

After breakfast Mary walked with Clarence to the front lobby of the Sanitarium. There the two young people bade each other farewell as Clarence had to catch the train going north, and Mary had to be on duty in the surgical department soon. This departure was a happier one because Clarence promised to write and come back in June to claim her as his bride.

*2. Mary's parents, Lafayette Haskell (May 5, 1843–February 2, 1928) and Margaret Stephens Haskell (October 7, 1843–December 16, 1922). Lafayette and Margaret were married on July 18, 1809.*

*3. Mary Haskell at twenty-three years of age. This photo was taken in 1897 after her first year of working as a colporteur in Iowa.*

*4. Clarence Rentfro and Mary with Charles and baby Marian.*

5. Mary at age forty-two with her three surviving children—Marian (age ten), Curtis (age seven), and Charles (age twelve).

6. Family photo with Mary's sister, Susan. Front row: Susan Haskell Wilbur and Mary. Middle row: Marian and Curtis.
Back row: Charles and Clarence.

*7. The last photo taken of Mary Haskell Rentfro.*

## Chapter 25
# *Preparing for Graduation and a Wedding*

When Mary arrived in the surgical department, she sang as she sterilized the surgical supplies of operating instruments, gloves, and bandages. Trays needed to be organized to be ready for operations. When surgery was in progress, Mary had to be there in the room standing beside the head surgeon, Dr. J.D. Shively, ready to answer his call for anything he needed.

After each day's work, Mary returned to her room to study and write letters to Clarence and to her sister, Susan, now a pioneer nurse to the Chinese nationals. These were times of loneliness for Mary, but the days brought new challenges of courage and trust in God. The days and hours slipped by as she threw herself into her nursing.

Mary took her nursing very seriously and tried to be as accurate as she could with all the procedures she learned. One time as she worked in the surgical department, she assisted a famous doctor from Chicago with a procedure. The surgery went fine, and the doctor announced, "We will close the wound now, Nurse."

"Oh, no, Doctor," Mary proclaimed. "We cannot. I'm missing a sponge."

"That's impossible, Miss Haskell," scoffed the doctor. "Count them again."

She did so. "A sponge is missing," insisted Mary. "Please, Doctor, open the wound and remove the sponge."

The doctor became irritated. "You are mistaken. There is no sponge in this patient."

"Please, Doctor," implored Mary. "Open the wound and remove the sponge."

"Well, Your Majesty," sneered the doctor, "I will open the wound and show that you are mistaken."

As he opened the wound, he saw a sponge, and the blood rushed to his face as he immediately became humble. "My apologies, Miss Haskell. Your expertise saved the life of this patient."

Mary continued to do her best each day. One day Dr. Shively said to Mary while getting ready to operate, "I didn't think Susan and Edwin would be called to China so soon. I thought it would be a long time in the future because the church people are not used to giving to foreign missions. We want to be more effective now. Dr. Emma Perrive and I will give you every advantage during the remaining months you're here so you'll be well prepared for foreign mission service in Spain."

True to their promise both doctors called Mary to accompany them on their house calls and to participate in office exams. They wanted her to be exposed to the recommended nursing care for the different ailments they diagnosed. Special instruction on the birth and care of infants and the care of mothers by Dr. Perrive proved interesting to Mary and would provide her with excellent experience for missionary work.

Mary's brother, Robert, knew that although she worked hard, she was very lonely without Susan, so one day much to her pleasure, he arrived at the Sanitarium to visit her. He observed some beautiful Concord grapes being delivered to the kitchen, so he asked if he could work out his stay by giving them a hand in preparing the grapes for canning. He got the job, and as other fruits came in, he continued to work until two months passed. Mary was her old happy self now with Robert there.

One day when Mary returned to her room, she found the long-looked-for letter from Susan. It was dated October 27, 1902, which said:

Dearest Sister Mary,

I can only write a short note this time. We arrived in China at last! We encountered a terrible storm at sea. It tested the courage of the bravest passengers, but God saw us all through. Soon we are to disembark. Our big challenge will be to find a place to live. Then, Edwin is anxious to find a Chinese teacher right away. As you know, Chinese is a very difficult language to speak, write, and

## Chapter 25  Preparing for Graduation and a Wedding   105

read. I shall write you as soon as we get settled. I'm sure you are eager to hear about the scenery, people, customs, and our experiences in reaching the hearts of the people.

How are you and Clarence? Do write and tell me all about yourself, your plans and about our beloved parents and brothers. I do miss them so. I do hope they too will yield their hearts to our loving Saviour to whom we have given our lives in service.

Let me hear from you, my loving sis, for I am lonesome for you. It just broke my heart to see you standing there on the station's platform all alone waving goodbye to us. I prayed that the Lord would watch over you, Sis, as you returned to the Sanitarium to your duties and studies.

I do hope to hear from you soon. I shall send you our address as soon as we find a place. We both love you.

Lovingly your sis,

Susan and Brother Ed

Once again tears flowed down Mary's cheeks as she folded her sister's letter. *I must let Robert read Susan's letter. Bless their hearts; I know that by now they must be on the mainland*, she thought.

However, another letter awaited her attention. Clarence wrote to tell

> *We arrived in China at last! We encountered a terrible storm at sea. It tested the courage of the bravest passengers, but God saw us all through.*

her that the Iowa Conference assigned him to work at Waverly, Iowa, for the winter months. This pleased Mary because she and Susan had sold many books there. He told her that he needed to prove himself as a soul winner. Professor Jefferson and Elder Moore planned to hold a tent effort there with Clarence's help. When finished he would join Elder W.H. Brinkerhoff and Elder McClintock at Kalona, Iowa. His main duties now were to instruct the interested people and get them ready for baptism.

Clarence continued to keep Mary informed about future plans so they could be prepared when their call came from the General Conference to enter mission service in Spain. Mary had plans of her own to develop now because two great events soon would take place—-first her graduation as a nurse, and next, her wedding to Clarence Rentfro. Mother Haskell had recently written to Mary and said:

> Please come home. I will help you with your wedding. It will be my greatest pleasure to have you married here at home. I will get the house ready for the wedding, guests will be invited, and food prepared. Just let me know the date, daughter.
>
> With much love,
>
> Your Mother

Mary stood by her window in solemn thought. Spring had come again with birds singing and flowers blooming, even the violets. Soon she would be leaving this haven of peace and training for the Master's call. Her thoughts whirled around like a dancing ballerina. *I have tried my best to perform my duties faithfully, not only here, but at home, and in the canvassing work. Now in a few days my graduation, and then my wedding to Clarence,* she mused. A long sigh escaped her lips.

The Iowa Conference officials invited Mary and Clarence to marry at campmeeting with two other couples, but Mary made her decision to be married at home for the sake of her mother.

*Chapter 26*
# The Wedding

When Mary's school term ended, she graduated, and the Sanitarium officials gave her a wonderful farewell. Mary packed her belongings and headed toward home with a stop off at campmeeting. Clarence was helping there, and when she arrived, Elder Spicer asked to see them regarding their prospects of going to Spain. He told them that Ellen G. White was in Europe and advised the General Conference to encourage young ministers to prepare for foreign mission work. He knew of Clarence's work in the field, but he needed to interview Mary.

When he asked Mary about her experience, she replied shyly, "I have only canvassed."

"How long did you stay in the canvassing work?" he asked her.

"Five and a half years," she replied.

"That is a good recommendation for a missionary," Elder Spicer said with a smile.

Clarence added, "And she just finished her three-year nursing course at the Iowa Sanitarium in Des Moines."

"That is even better," Elder Spicer responded glowing with admiration. "You will be hearing from the General Conference Committee although we can't set a date yet. I also understand you two will be married soon. I think, Clarence, that you should follow the plans the Iowa Conference has for you, but be prepared to leave for Spain sometime next year. God bless you both in your new life partnership."

At the end of the conversation, Mary left for home, and Clarence went to work there at the campgrounds. "There is so much to think about," Mary said to herself as she traveled home. Her thoughts raced about Clarence, home, the wedding, and missionary service.

When Mary finally arrived home, she felt pleased to find everyone excited for her. Mother Haskell felt so proud to see her younger daughter as a full-fledged nurse now. Mary went over all the wedding details that were prepared by Mother and Father Haskell, Robert, and older brother, Marshall. The parlor would be decorated with ferns from the nearby woods and pink roses from the rose arbor in the flower garden beside the house. The wedding refreshments and meals were all planned. One of the neighbors even planned to bring ice cream for the occasion. A long table overlaid with a freshly starched tablecloth, centered with a vase of pink roses and silverware, would be set in place for each guest. Vases of ferns and roses in each room would produce a sweet fragrance welcoming all to the wedding. Everything sounded beautiful and ready to go.

Clarence, his mother, and his youngest brother arrived at the Haskell home to attend the wedding leaving his father home to do chores. Relatives by the dozen came on June 11, 1903, the special day. Anna Stevenson, a schoolmate, played the wedding music on the home organ as Father Haskell proudly escorted his beautiful younger daughter down to the front of a lovely arch decorated with ferns and pink roses. Waiting for them at the front stood Elder L. F. Starr, the Iowa Conference president, who would perform the marriage, along with a tall, handsome, young bridegroom, Clarence Emerson Rentfro.

The beautiful wedding proceeded, and after the ceremony, the couple enjoyed a pleasant reception. As the guests began to leave, Mary and Clarence went out to the veranda and looked over the front yard to the barn and out to the road. What a sight greeted their eyes—all about were carriages and buggies of various sizes with lots of neighing horses wanting to go home to eat.

As the last guest said goodbye, Clarence turned to Mary and said, "Let's tell our parents at the supper table about our visit with Elder Spicer at campmeeting."

"That's a good idea, Clarence," she responded as she looked up into the face of her new husband. "Wasn't Mother wonderful and kind through all this excitement? How proud she looked as she stood there receiving all the guests!"

Clarence agreed and slipped his arm around Mary's tiny waist to draw her close to him. They looked out into the apple orchard full of trees

## Chapter 26  The Wedding

loaded with pink apple blossoms so beautiful against the blue horizon with the sunset glow ushering in evening shadows.

Then, Mary pointed to the sky and said, "Look, Clarence, see that star over yonder!"

"Yes," he responded. "What about it?"

"Why it's even brighter tonight than ever before," she exclaimed.

"It always shines that bright, but I know what you mean." Then Clarence began to sing "Will There Be Any Stars in My Crown?" And their thoughts turned to the years ahead wondering if they would ever get to Spain.

They went back into the house to see if Elder Starr was ready to go to the station at Garwin. Elder Starr affirmed that he needed to go and said, "Clarence, I heard you singing a beautiful song outside. I like your tenor voice."

Thanking him for the compliment, Clarence announced that he and Mary would take him to the station. "But, wait just a moment," Mary said, "I need to change, so I won't spoil my pretty wedding dress."

She returned shortly dressed in a dark brown dress trimmed in white French applique' and a lovely white hat that Susan had made for her a number of years ago.

Elder Starr commented when she returned, "That is the fastest change I have ever seen from a young lady. You've proven you can do things efficiently." The three of them walked to the buggy with Blanche all harnessed and ready to trot off to the station.

Just before Elder Starr departed on the train back to his office, he told the couple that he would be waiting to see how the summer went. Clarence confirmed that he would keep in touch.

When Mary and Clarence returned from the station, Mother Haskell had supper ready for them. As they ate together, Clarence related Elder Spicer's conversation regarding his consideration of them for mission service. Mother Haskell realized her younger daughter was giving her life in service for the Master. She began crying as though her heart would break. In her mind she thought, *Oh, if I had not been so hard and cruel and said so many unkind words to my lovely daughter years ago, perhaps she wouldn't have the desire to leave home and go so far away. They might have lived near me so I could see my grandchildren.* The once hardened heart of Mother Haskell had changed now, but it was too late to entice her daughter away from the vision of serving Christ in foreign lands. Her daughter was with her now, but in her heart, she knew it would not be for long.

"Oh, dear!" she cried out. "How can I ever make it up to you and Susan for the way I acted toward you both?" Mary and Clarence signaled to each other to rise from their chairs and go to Mother's side to comfort her. Mary slipped her arms around her mother's neck as she whispered comforting words to help her feel better.

"Let's forget the past. God will forgive you, and I hold no hard feelings because of it," Mary consoled. Mother Haskell wiped the tears from her eyes, raised her head, and looked into her daughter's eyes, noticing tears in them, too. The two embraced each other in a true, loving clasp for the first time since she was a small girl attending Sabbath School and church.

Lovingly she told Mary, "Darling, I love you dearly. It was my selfish heart that treated you so cruelly, so please forgive me, dear, for the many unkind words, actions, and the hateful way I treated you and your sister when you wanted to follow the Adventist truths and all they believed. I know now that God had His hands in all your plans. Go, serve your Master. I shall be a better mother from now on to you girls as long as I live."

It took courage for Mother Haskell to say those words in the presence of others at the table. She knew there was something more than religion in her daughter's heart to give up the luxuries of her life for poor living conditions and to be with a strange-speaking people and a strange culture. To sacrifice their lives to bring the Adventist religion to the people over there in far-off lands showed her the bravery of both of her girls.

*Chapter 27*
# *Working for the Lord*

After two days at home, Mary and Clarence left for their summer's work to assist Professor Jefferson of the Stewart Seventh-day Adventist Academy for a while. From there the Rentfros moved on to Algona to be with Elder B. L. Dieffenbacher at his tent meetings. Later the Iowa Conference Committee sent Clarence to an eastern town in the state to conduct evangelistic meetings for about three months. This was a time of testing Clarence's ability as a good worker to preach the gospel and win souls to Christ.

Winter began with a vengeance. Snow fell covering the fields with white blankets and painting lace doilies on the trees and buildings. Roads and trees glistened with ice, and icicles clambered down from rooftops. The severe weather plunged thermometers way below freezing with its bitter cold.

However, people braved the cold and met at night in a heated schoolhouse out in a rural district among farmers in a Catholic community. Filling the place to capacity each night, Clarence preached to many interested people eager to learn a new way of living. Usually, at meetings of this type, there are some who come because of their interest. A few come just to hear a young pastor preach about the Bible in their community. Some come out of curiosity, a few come for fun, and others come for mischief.

The mischief-makers were often young men who came with the intent of breaking up religious meetings. One cold night while Clarence preached, nails began flying in all directions making noise as they hit the floor. Some of the nails landed on the listeners making them jump and turn around to see who did that. No one could detect the culprit, and nails pinged as they fell on the floor, and people kept jumping when hit. Not only was the noise distressing, but some of the listeners began to panic. Mary, who stood by the entrance, saw this commotion. With her roving, brown eyes, she quickly caught the ringleader in the very act of throwing the nails.

Stepping quickly and quietly to the side of the ringleader she whispered, "Son, please keep those nails in your pocket."

The nail throwing ceased, but Mary did not relax her vigilance. The ringleader saw that her eyes were not about to move from him, so he decided to leave. That settled the disturbance for the night.

During the day Clarence and Mary drove out to the country homes inviting the farmers to attend the meetings at the schoolhouse. They also distributed tracts, visited interested people, and gave Bible studies. Attendance at the night meetings ranged from seventy-five to 140 depending on the winter weather.

One Sunday evening a crowd even larger than usual attended the meeting. Snow fell all day packing down on the roads making travel by sleigh the preferred method of arriving. Everyone seemed to be in excellent spirits even though it was very cold outside. As people entered the schoolhouse, they quietly took their seats while Clarence played sacred songs on his violin.

Mary welcomed people at the entrance, but once when she went to seat others, she glanced back at the door to see a group of farmers dressed in overalls enter and walk right to the front row to seat themselves. They listened attentively to every word spoken during the sermon. When the audience stood to sing the last song, the farmers arose and left the building. This alerted Clarence and made him think, *Now we are in for trouble.* So, at that very moment, he sent a silent prayer to his Heavenly Father to send angels to be with Mary and himself during the rest of the evening.

Mary also prayed when she saw the farmers leave. *Dear Lord, please send help right now to protect Your servants from whatever may happen. May Your truth and power be shown here tonight to the neighbors as a result of this meeting. I thank You, Lord. Amen.*

Accompanied by Clarence with his violin and with his tenor voice, the closing song sounded so beautiful. He offered a prayer, then went to the door to shake hands with the people as they left and invite them to return for the next meeting. Everyone appeared to be happy as they left and expressed pleasantries to the young pastor. Mary began straightening the room while Clarence checked the windows and closed the drafts of the wood heater so it would not burn while they were gone.

Next Clarence and Mary walked out of the door, and Clarence turned to close the door behind them. When he turned back, he and Mary started down the schoolhouse steps surprised by the presence of the farmers forming a line on each side of the path from the door to the road.

Clarence grabbed Mary's arm and whispered in her ear, "We'll walk briskly and quietly between them to our horse and buggy. There is no other way to go."

The Rentfros could not afford a sleigh, so they had used their buggy even though it was dangerous on the icy roads. Their horse was tied to the hitching post beside the road near the path to the schoolhouse.

Not a word was spoken by either one as they walked quietly down the path between the overall-clad farmers to their waiting horse and buggy. As soon as the couple reached their high-spirited horse and began to untie the reins, without warning, a pail of ice water showered Clarence.

The ruffians of the nail throwing episode had returned and were waiting for the preacher behind the buggy beside the road to take him by surprise. In an instant the farmers equipped with long sticks from the nearby willow trees took off in pursuit of the ruffians. The next sound was yelling and crying as the farmers took care of the ruffians.

> *In an instant the farmers equipped with long sticks from the nearby willow trees took off in pursuit of the ruffians. The next sound was yelling and crying as the farmers took care of the ruffians.*

The neighbor across the road from the schoolhouse heard all the noise and rushed over to find poor Clarence all wet and shivering from the dousing. The water immediately turned to ice due to the frigid temperature and made him look like an icicle. Taking one look, the neighbor urged, "Hurry over to my house right over there, and I'll make sure you get dry clothes as soon as I finish looking around here. Mrs. Wills and I welcome you both to spend the night at our home."

Clarence and Mary expressed their gratitude to their benefactor. They accepted his kind invitation to spend the night with them in their farmhouse. Mr. Wills also led the Rentfros' horse, Dan, to the barn, unhitched him, and fed him a good dinner of hay and oats before putting him in a comfortable stall.

The Wills seemed pleased to have the privilege of hosting the young pastor and his wife for the night. Dry clothes replaced the wet ones that were hung to dry during the night. Before retiring, the four discussed the events of the evening. Clarence asked, "Who were those farmers?"

Mr. Wills replied, "I never saw them before tonight. I did see them come into the meeting and sit down in the front row. Then I saw them get up and leave, but I didn't see them outside when I left for home."

Clarence suddenly understood the situation. He turned to Mary and their hosts and said, "Let's kneel before the Lord and thank our Heavenly Father for His loving protection. He sent His angels dressed as farmers to protect us from further harm. Let's pray that this experience will stir the hearts of the people all around the community."

The following day Clarence visited the Catholic priest of the community relating to him the experience of his ice water bath. The priest paid intense attention to the young pastor and promised his cooperation in keeping peace in his parish. After that visit, there were no more disturbances at the meetings.

However, as a result of the icy shower and his deliverance, Clarence felt more energized at the meetings which resulted in fourteen souls baptized at the end of the three-month effort. The Wills who had befriended Clarence and Mary that cold night were among the group baptized. The new Adventists organized into a church with the help of the Iowa Conference president, L. F. Starr. That church continued to be a light in the community.

## Chapter 28
## *On Their Way*

When spring finally arrived, Clarence and Mary returned to Clarence's parental home on the farm in Sigourney to relax for a time. On March 18, 1904, a baby boy named Charles arrived in the family. This baby did not lack attention due to his four uncles, two aunts, and grandparents who all tended to spoil him.

With their vacation over on June 3, Clarence, Mary, and Charles headed to campmeeting at Colfax. Also present at the campmeeting were Elder W. A. Spicer, secretary of the General Conference and the Foreign Mission Board, plus Elder A. G. Daniels, president of the General Conference. These were the men who received applications from both Clarence and Mary before their marriage requesting an opportunity to serve in Spain. Now the couple received an invitation to visit with Elder Spicer at the foreign mission tent.

At that meeting Elder Spicer asked Clarence, "Are you still willing to leave your home here for a home and life of service in Spain?"

This seemed to be an easy question for Clarence to answer since he had long dreamed of being a missionary to Spain. Without any hesitation he answered, "Yes, if the Lord is willing."

Elder Spicer then turned to Mary and said, "I understand you now have a baby to add to your happiness. Are you willing to leave the comforts of living here for a life of foreign service which possibly includes hardships and inconveniences like in Spain?"

"Oh, yes," Mary responded with enthusiasm. "This is what I always wanted ever since my canvassing experiences."

The young couple then listened solemnly as Elder Spicer explained that the Foreign Mission Board Committee of the General Conference authorized him to present them an official invitation to go to Spain. Anticipating the next question, both Clarence and Mary held their breath until Elder Spicer asked. "Are you both now willing to go to Spain?"

Mary reached over and squeezed Clarence's hand as he answered for both of them, "We gladly accept this kind invitation of the Foreign Mission Board to go to Spain, the land of our dreams, to spread this wonderful gospel message."

With deep emotion Elder Spicer said, "Let's have a consecration prayer to God for you as you devote your service to Him leaving home and loved ones to help fulfill Christ's great command, 'Go ye into all the world.'" With that the three of them bowed in prayer in sincere consecration.

After the prayer came the next question from Elder Spicer, "How soon would you be ready to leave?"

"As soon as the Foreign Mission Board sends word, we will be ready to go," asserted Clarence.

They were assured that it would take a few months to make all the arrangements, and the leaders needed to solicit funds at other campmeetings to carry out these plans. Thus ended the most important meeting of the lives of this young couple.

As soon as campmeeting finished on June 13, the Rentfros went to hold a tent effort at North English located northeast of Sigourney. Attendance was good at the meetings with from forty-five to 140 people coming. Clarence and Mary kept busy visiting, handing out fliers, selling books, and having a health exhibition. An organized church eventually resulted because of these meetings.

On July 2 the Rentfros received their official call to mission service. How excited they felt to read the letter! Clarence preached his farewell sermon at Sigourney. They bought Spanish books, a dictionary, and a geography book to study the country, people and language to prepare themselves for their dream work for God in Spain.

Big questions pummeled their minds. What will it be like to live in Spain? Would the people be friendly? Would they be able to find a home? No one knew the answers because no one had ever gone as missionaries to Spain before from the Adventist Church. Soon they would find the answers for themselves.

## Chapter 28  On Their Way

To prepare further for their trip and for living in Spain, Mary needed to sew items to take with them besides purchasing others. The Foreign Mission Board cautioned them to travel lightly to reduce expenses, so they took the advice seriously and complied with the request.

In the meantime, Clarence received a letter from his sister Bess Rentfro Hawkins and brother-in-law, William, who were studying at Washington Missionary College in Washington, D.C., telling him they had received an invitation to go to China as missionaries. They, too, were getting ready to leave soon. This news pleased Clarence and delighted Mary who observed, "Now, we each have a missionary sister in China."

As they packed their trunks and boxes, they placed a label on each that read—C. E. Rentfro, Barcelona, Spain, Europe. Sometimes they would just stand and look at the labels hardly believing it was true that they would soon be in Spain. Then, the train tickets from Sigourney to New York City and the boat passage overseas to London and on to Spain arrived in the mail.

Soon the time came to say goodbye first to Clarence's family and then to the Haskells who drove all the way from Garwin in their buggy pulled by Blanche. Mother dreaded saying her last farewell to Mary and her family. She and Father also wanted to meet Charles since they had not seen their new grandson yet. What a grand time they had together during the short visit.

The soon-to-be missionaries felt sad about leaving home but thrilled that they were about to leave for the land of their youthful dreams. Soon it would all be a reality. All the members of both families accompanied Clarence and Mary to the train station. They knew the possibility existed that they would never see the young couple again, so tears glistened in more than a few eyes as the train pulled into the station.

After they boarded and the train began chugging off away from the families, they waved their handkerchiefs until all were out of sight. Clarence, Mary, and Charles found a seat in the coach as they headed for New York City. Charles fell asleep in Mary's arms, and Clarence went out on the platform to watch the countryside fly by. He felt nostalgic as he saw the familiar farms and landscapes pass out of his vision. Cattle grazing in the fields, crops growing in the fertile soil, wooded hills here and there beside a shining blue river with a bridge made him feel a little sad. "I won't be seeing these scenes for a long time," he mused. He finally said goodbye to his familiar landmarks and returned to join his little family.

"How is my missionary nurse?" he said to Mary as he sat down by her. Little Charles slept contentedly in her arms as she watched the scenery out of the window.

She smiled at him and said, "Just fine feeling comfortable in God's care. Clarence ..." she started to ask him a question.

"Yes, dear," he replied in a distracted manner.

Mary pursued the conversation. "I'm so glad Mother came with Robert and Father to see us off. That way she met your family. You know she bitterly opposed Susan and me as we became deeply involved in this message. She did all in her power to destroy our faith in God and our devotion to His Word. For a while the oppression became so great that sometimes we felt like giving up. If it had not been for God's help and Susan's strength it would have been easy to slip back into her way of living, but we stayed strong. I'm glad Mother's heart has softened toward us. We may never see our parents again on this earth. I only hope it won't be too late for them to give their hearts wholly to God because I long for them to be with us in heaven. Let's pray to God to keep them in His care while we are absent from them in a foreign land spreading the seed of God's Word."

They both bowed their heads in prayer at that very moment.

When the train arrived in Chicago, they stopped for the weekend to visit friends and went to church with them on Sabbath besides spending a pleasant afternoon with them at one of the zoos. Next, they traveled by boat from Chicago north to Benton Harbor, Michigan, and on to Berrien Springs. While there they found they could pick plums and pears in exchange for a place to stay. What fun they had picking and eating the fruit.

The college at Berrien Springs seemed to be undergoing a building program. From there they rode by train to Battle Creek where they were guests of Dr. John Kellogg at the magnificent Battle Creek Sanitarium. While there, they attended church at the Battle Creek Tabernacle on September 7, 1904, and were privileged to see and listen to Ellen G. White preach. What an inspiration and wonderful privilege for the Rentfros! It helped renew their courage for the great task of being missionaries in a strange land for Christ.

Early on Sunday morning the Rentfros left Battle Creek by train for Niagara Falls and thrilled at the sight of the beautiful roaring waters as they came rushing past. From Niagara Falls they rode the train to New York City where they were met at Grand Central Station by the Seventh-day Adventist transportation travel agent, Brother Calvert, whose job consisted of assisting all missionaries leaving and entering the United

## Chapter 28  On Their Way

States. After helping them shop for necessary articles, he accompanied them to the dock where the steamship floated in the harbor.

On September 10, 1904, at 9:30 a.m., the Rentfros embarked on the steamship *Philadelphia* to sail across the Atlantic Ocean to London, England. Clarence, Mary, and baby Charles stood on the upper deck to wave goodbye to their only friend, Brother Calvert, as the steamer glided out of the port on its way to the rolling ocean. As they passed the Statue of Liberty with her arm upraised lifting high the torch, she looked as though she, too, were waving goodbye to the foreign missionaries who were leaving their homeland to live in a foreign country for a season.

# Section III

*Chapter 29*

# An Arrival Shock

The couple felt seasick the first few days because of the rolling motion of the ship, but when they felt better, they explored the ship. Then it began raining, so Clarence spent the days reading, but Mary visited with some of the ladies and gave them Bible studies. After a few days, the rain stopped, and the pleasant weather encouraged the couple to pass out tracts to their passenger friends. They gave the ship's nurse the book, *Christ's Object Lessons.* A concert in the lounge room entertained them one afternoon.

On September 17 the ship stopped at Plymouth then went on to South Hampton near London to drop anchor. Upon disembarking they went into London and rode a carriage to the English Seventh-day Adventist Conference Office to meet with Elder W. C. Sisley, president.

In the meantime, Elder Sisley had received a cablegram from Elder A. G. Daniels in Battle Creek addressed to Clarence, which he handed to him when they met. They both wondered at its contents.

> *Upon opening the cablegram, Clarence read the message and immediately turned pale and trembled. It read, "Rentfro—Portugal."*

## Chapter 29 An Arrival Shock

Upon opening the cablegram, Clarence read the message and immediately turned pale and trembled. It read, "Rentfro—Portugal."

Mary stood beside Clarence and noticed the sudden change come over her husband. "What's wrong?" she inquired.

"Read it," he exclaimed as he handed the cablegram to her. As Mary read the message, her big brown eyes opened wide with great surprise.

She turned to Clarence and asked, "What are we going to do?"

He answered in an eerily calm voice, "The Rentfros are going to Portugal."

Elder Sisley, too, was surprised to read the two-word cablegram which would change the lives of the young couple. However, he did tell them that a few weeks before, two brothers named Bond from California studying at Stanborough College in London had expressed their desire to go to Spain and were now on their way there with their families.

Nevertheless, it was a great shock to the Rentfros who had planned for so many years to serve in Spain. They had studied the language, culture, and geography of that country, and now all their plans and dreams were shattered due to the message in the cablegram. They could hardly believe their eyes, but as they re-read the message, they knew there was no mistake.

So, with determined resignation, the couple ordered new labels to be addressed like this: C. E. Rentfro, Lisbon, Portugal, Europe.

A new and greater task now lay ahead for Mary and Clarence as they accepted the turn of events as part of God's plan for them. As soon as possible Clarence located a bookstore in London and purchased a Portuguese-English dictionary and a Portuguese Bible so he could begin studying the new language. Next, he went back to the station to put the new labels on their baggage. Then, he sent a cable to President Daniels which read: "To Portugal we go!"

On Friday, September 23, the Rentfros left London by train for South Hampton, and at noon they boarded the Portuguese steamship, *Madalena*, bound for Lisbon, Portugal. Slowly the ship pulled out of port and headed into the ocean toward Lisbon.

The Rentfros spent the first days on the ship quietly studying the books they had purchased. They gave away tracts to several people. When the ship stopped at Vigo in northwest Spain, they bought some peaches from merchants on the dock while passing out some of their stock of Spanish tracts to people there.

On September 24, sixteen days from the time they left the United States, their ship dropped anchor a distance from the coast and the city of

Lisbon. The Rentfros went up on deck to gaze at the sights of the country where they would live and spread the gospel.

As they looked along the horizon, they could see sailboats and other vessels. A fisherman's brightly painted boat glided past them on its way to the sea. "I wonder what it's going to be like living here," Mary remarked to Clarence. "We don't know anything about Portugal."

"I believe the Portuguese earn their living by fishing," responded Clarence. "Remember, Mary, when we were in elementary school, our geography books said the Portuguese sailors sailed the Atlantic and Pacific to discover new lands. Fishing fleets still roam the ocean hunting for schools of sardines. They also fish for cod to supply the world."

If Clarence could have recalled the history of the Golden Decades, he might have realized that Portugal became an independent nation under its first king—Don Joao I. During the fifteenth and sixteenth centuries, called the Golden Decades, Portugal became an empire and ruled half of the then-known world under the leadership of Prince Henry the Navigator. Some of the famous Portuguese explorers were Bartolomeu Dias who sailed to the Cape of Good Hope on the tip of Africa, Vasco da Gama who sailed around the Cape to India, Pedro Alvares Cabral who discovered Brazil, and Ferdinand Magellan who became the first to sail around the world.

A geography book would have informed them that the country is at the tip edge of Europe and is not much larger than the state of Maine. It is about 295 miles long and eighty-eight miles wide with a long coastline of 1,114 miles. The only country bordering it is Spain. The northern part is mostly mountains and hills while the southern part is rolling plains to a coastal plain. The coastline is mostly composed of limestone caves and grottoes, but there are places to swim in the Atlantic Ocean.

Two major events caused problems for the country. These were the 1755 earthquake that destroyed Lisbon and the Napoleonic wars in 1803–1815, which resulted in Portugal losing its largest colony—Brazil.

When the Rentfros arrived in 1904, there were two-lane roads from Minho Province in the north down to the beach in beautiful Algarve in the south. The country had become famous for its sardines, cork, and Madeira wines. There were neat compulsory primary schools in every village and many Catholic churches. As a patriarchal society with ancient extremes of poverty and wealth, many cultural customs existed. For example, when a fisherman walked on the road, his smiling wife walked behind him balancing a basket of goodies on her head.

## Chapter 29  An Arrival Shock

Eager to get on land, Clarence and Mary soon discovered that they needed to board a smaller boat to get to shore because the ship could not navigate around the rocks in the harbor. The rocks resting there resulted from the Lisbon earthquake. Soon they boarded the launch, and it made its way toward the coast where they could see a hill with many houses perching on it like colorful dollhouses on a patchwork quilt.

"Another fishing boat just passed by," exclaimed Mary as she pointed it out to Clarence. "Why there's another one, and look—more are still coming, and all are heading out to sea. You are right about the Portuguese being men of the sea. Just look at all those happy fishermen as they all sail by. How will we ever reach the hearts of those men who put out to sea every day of the year?" Mary sighed.

"God will find a way, my dear," assured Clarence. "It won't be easy, but there will be a way. You'll see. God will help us reach at least one fisherman's heart." Then with his dictionary in his hand, he continued, "I must learn some Portuguese words so I can communicate with folks when we reach the port."

"How do you say good morning?" asked Mary.

"Hmm. Here it is. *Bom Dia*," said Clarence.

"Let me find my pencil," said Mary as she searched in her pocket. "I'm going to write down a list of words and phrases. You look up the meanings in Portuguese, and I will write the translation beside the list." So Mary made a list of common words and phrases, so they could get along until they found a Portuguese teacher.

"Here comes the launch," announced Mary, "I will wake Charles up from his nap while you get our suitcases."

The launch sent to guide them past the rocky shoals into the *Rio Tejo* (Tagus River) mouth which forms the wide bay of Lisbon soon brought them to fresh waters. Now the Rentfros could see the port easily with all the people milling about. The men were dressed in colorful checked shirts, baggy trousers, high boots, and stocking caps. In the long stocking caps, they kept their money and other valuables. Some of the people were dark-skinned like the invading Moors, and others were blonde as Visigoths. Mary admired the brilliant outfits of the women with their colorful skirts, white lace blouses, and bare feet. Most of them carried large baskets on their heads.

As the ship started to drop anchor, they could hear the people shouting and singing out their wares. "Peixe fresco!" Quickly Clarence referred to his dictionary looking under the letter P to see what they shouted about.

"What is it they're selling, Clarence?" inquired Mary.

"Here it is," exclaimed Clarence finding the words in his Portuguese dictionary. "Those women are selling fresh fish. See that woman walking erect carrying a basket on her head. She is pulling out a big fish from it. I even see some children carrying loads upon their heads, too."

"How can they walk so straight with things on their heads?" wondered Mary. "I see something rolled up under the basket. It's round and sits on their heads. I wonder how they make that. Perhaps when we learn the language, we can ask someone about how it all works."

"That's a good idea," agreed Clarence. Then he pointed to a man leading a donkey with two baskets straddled across its back loaded with large bundles of dry grass-like materials. "I wonder what that is for."

"Just think," said Mary. "This picturesque country will be our adopted country for a long time. Now, I'm anxious to step on solid ground again. I think the boat is stopping."

"Why it has!" grinned Clarence. "Look, the gangplank is being lowered. We are home at last. Our new dream has come true."

*Chapter 30*

# Here at Last

On September 26, 1904, the first Seventh-day Adventist foreign missionaries to Portugal walked down the gangplank onto Portuguese soil. As soon as they descended they were surrounded by people shouting out their wares.

"What a fishy smell!" complained Mary.

"Oh, look at all those baskets of sardines," said Clarence. "There must be thousands of sardines in those baskets."

The fish were all sorted by size. Large, small, and even smaller fish lay out in open baskets in the hot sun in row upon row. The smell was stifling. Each person must own a basket for so many were calling the same thing, "*Psst, psst! Senhor e senhora. Venha aqui. Peixe fresco!*" (Man and woman. Come here. Fresh fish!)

The people seemed friendly to the foreigners coming to their shores, but no one came to meet the Rentfros. They were not alone, however, for they knew the Lord guided them on the voyage, and He would assist them in working in this strange land. They bowed their heads and thanked God for their safe arrival in Lisbon. After passing through inspection, they walked out of the Custom House gate with their suitcases and baby Charles and stood on the street with a puzzled look on their faces.

"Which way shall we go?" asked Clarence.

Mary thought a moment looking this way and that way. Her canvassing days flashed through her mind as she remembered walking miles at times looking for a place to stay. She could do that now, but with suitcases and a baby and not knowing the language, it could be a stupendous task. Her eye caught a glimpse of some stairs to her right leading to the upper level of the city. "Let's walk up those stairs. Maybe we might find a room to rent or perhaps a hotel," she suggested.

Lisbon is built on a steep hill. Instead of roads, stairs go from one level to another. In some sections of the city, cable cars carried people up and down. Children often played on the steps instead of in the streets. Women sunned themselves on the steps or did the family wash while visiting a friend or a neighbor.

Clarence agreed to Mary's plan to go up the steps. As they climbed to the next level, they saw so many houses with colorful blue tiles on the outside walls. They discovered that these tiles were characteristic of Portugal, and were found on dishes and other items. The houses seemed to have many iron balconies surrounding the windows. Although these houses were almost a thousand years old, they were still solid with firm foundations and blue tile roofs.

The missionaries who were still looking for a place to stay decided to try the next set of stairs to the second level. When they reached the top, Clarence asked, "Shall we turn to the left?"

"Let's do," answered Mary. "The view is just beautiful from this level."

People gazed at them as they passed by and said, "Sao Americanos." The missionaries understood those words. Other people passing would stare at them. Women would say, "*O, bebe e lindo. Sao Americanos. O homen tem carinho parece bondoso*" (Oh, a beautiful baby. They are Americans. The man seems affectionate and kind). One lady caressed the baby as she passed by showing friendliness toward the little family.

Mary said aloud, "Oh, you dear people! You are trying to make us feel welcome here in this country that is strange and new to us. Someday we will be able to speak with you. Give us time, and we will do it."

The missionaries continued to walk and look for signs that might indicate rooms were available. Suddenly Mary spied a large sign in the window. "I wonder what it says."

Clarence took the dictionary from his coat pocket and began hunting for the words, *Casa Para Alugar* (House for Rent). He turned to the Cs and looked up that word, then proceeded to look up the other words. "Aha! It means House for Rent. Now we are getting somewhere." Clarence wrote down the name and address of the landlord. After locating the man, they found they would have to wait a few days before they could move in. The man told them where to find the English hotel.

A cart man drove by, so Clarence flagged him down and loaded their baggage on the cart as they walked toward the hotel. When they arrived, Clarence saw a sign in the lobby that read "English is spoken here." So, he spoke in English to the manager, but the manager replied, *"Nao posso falar em ingles"* (I cannot speak in English).

Clarence frowned and pointed to the sign. The man shook his head *No*. So, once again Clarence took his dictionary from his pocket. He eventually rented a room for a few days until the house became available. After settling Mary and Charles, Clarence went back to the ship to retrieve their trunks and a large box. After that he went back to make arrangements with the landlord of the house for one month's rent. Much to his dismay the landlord shook his head and held up three fingers. He wanted three months' rent in advance. Clarence's financial supply would be nearly exhausted if he paid it. How would they live until the General Conference could send his monthly salary? He knew that even his salary would not be much. However, they needed a place to live, so he paid the rent.

He had enough money left to purchase a small square black iron charcoal stove, two wooden chairs, a simple small table, a broom, and some food like bread, beans, eggs, olive oil, fruit, and nuts. Then the money was gone.

"What will we do next?" he wondered. They had no friends in Portugal to whom they could go for assistance. Clarence sold his cow, calf, horse, and buggy equipment before leaving Iowa. The buyers wanted to pay with installments. If only they would send him the rest of the money they owed, that would help. He decided to write to them.

Since the General Conference sent them overseas, he expected they would send his salary since they knew where they were located. However, the General Conference was expecting the Iowa Conference to continue sending Clarence his monthly allowance until their treasury was better established. The members of the fairly new church organization were not into stable systematic giving, and the members were not yet foreign mission conscious. These plans needed yet to be taught, and officials needed to explain their value and necessity.

The Rentfros rested at the English hotel as they waited the two days until their house would be ready. They took time to go sightseeing in picturesque Lisbon by walking with Clarence pushing baby Charles in a type of folding stroller that they had purchased in New York City.

As they walked along, people stared at them, shrugged their shoulders, and some even poked fun at them. Not knowing the language and culture, Clarence and Mary wondered if something was really wrong.

An incident occurred with a man who drove a pair of goats carrying large cans strapped on their backs. Clarence and Mary observed the man crouching down by one of the goats with a tin cup and milking the goat. He opened a large can filled with water and dipped enough water out of the can to fill the rest of the tin cup. This diluted goat milk was offered to Clarence to drink as the man held up two fingers indicating the amount of money he wanted for the drink. Clarence shook his head No, so the man threw the drink out on the ground.

A lovely woman walked past them carrying a large basket on her head. She reached up inside the basket with her right hand bringing down a long, round, hard-crusted delicious-smelling loaf of bread. The smell broke down Mary's resistance, so she purchased it with the few coins in her pocket.

The way the women carried large baskets on their heads still fascinated Mary. She learned later that little children began learning to balance baskets on their heads by practicing with smaller baskets as they walked beside their erect mothers.

"I shall just have to start practicing carrying baskets on my head," she told Clarence, "because that is the style here."

"Oh, see that man! He's driving a donkey while sitting astride a large barrel strapped around the animal's back and belly. Wonder what he's selling. Let's find out!" Mary said as she motioned to the man.

He understood the sign and stopped by the couple. She discovered he sold olive oil, so he measured out some into a liter bottle for a few *reis*. They also saw a load of cork up ahead on a cart pulled by oxen whose huge horns nearly spanned the narrow street. Those walking by merely raised the horns up and out of the way, ducked under, and continued walking. This did not seem to bother the oxen.

Soon they came to an open market with various types of pottery jugs, colorful pitchers, and dishes of all sizes displayed on the ground. Women walked barefoot among these articles admiring them. They dressed in heavy dark skirts with white lace blouses topped with colorful capes and brilliant scarves on their heads and tied under their chins. Some of them

## Chapter 30  Here at Last

also carried baskets on their heads as they looked around and stepped over the pottery on the ground without dropping a thing. The scene amazed Mary.

"Look at those dark rain clouds rolling in over the ocean. We'd better return to our room before the storm hits us so far from the hotel," declared Clarence. So the sightseers called it a day and turned back, weary but happy to learn more about their new country.

As they prepared for the night, they heard mournful tones coming from outside. They opened their window to listen to the strange sounds wafting on the night air. Soon they heard the sounds of marching feet on the cobblestone streets. As the sound came closer and closer, they saw rows upon rows of men carrying long nets on their shoulders. They decided the men were the fishermen bringing their great nets ashore to keep them safe from the storm. They were chanting the song of the sea after a day's work.

After gazing out of the window watching the fishermen march by, Mary busied herself looking through the provisions Clarence had purchased earlier. She soon noticed that he had made no provision for a bed in their new house. "Clarence, what are we going to sleep on?"

In response he assured her that he would make a very comfortable bed for them. When she asked him how and out of what, he answered, "You'll see, dear."

After another day of resting and sightseeing, the Rentfros looked forward to moving into their first Portugal home located across from Jardin d' Estrela (now Jardim de Estrela).

*Chapter 31*

# *Learning How to Live in Lisbon*

The next day the Rentfros called a cart to haul their baggage over to their newly rented house. They spent the day unpacking and arranging what they could. They spent the night sleeping on the floor. The next day Clarence went to a nearby store and bought two round poles. He started carrying them home on his shoulders when he surprisingly received a warning from a policeman who told him that gentlemen must not carry things like that on the shoulders. Although he made it home, he received many stares from the natives.

Arriving home, he picked up the tape measure and saw to cut the poles into four equal legs. Next, he took apart the boards crating the trunks and large box. Out of them he fashioned the frame for the bed. For springs he used the rope that had been tied around the trunks and box and wound it tightly around the frame.

Mary decided to get in the act and found a tick made out of heavy striped cloth in the luggage and made a pillowcase as big as a mattress. But, how would they stuff it? Clarence remembered the farmer they saw from the deck of the ship with the donkey carrying dry material, so he went out to look for him. He brought along a piece of paper with his request for straw written in Portuguese. The man read it and nodded cheerfully, so Clarence took him to the house and gave him the tick to fill. The farmer left with the tick, and Clarence, somewhat apprehensive, hoped he would return.

## Chapter 31  Learning How to Live in Lisbon

That evening Clarence and Mary stepped out onto their balcony to look for the farmer who had their tick. Soon they spied him walking slowly along leading his donkey. Straddled across its back was the full tick bouncing along. What a happy sight to the young couple. It also made them laugh to see their mattress looking like a blown-up balloon taking a ride on the donkey's back nearly hiding the poor animal from sight.

They hurried downstairs to meet and pay the man and receive their mattress. Mary gave him a few reis from her supply of carefully saved money that was slowly being depleted. Then he and Clarence struggled upstairs carrying the awkward mattress and finally placed it on the frame. Mary inspected it and decided it didn't look too bad on the frame, and in fact, it looked rather cozy. They were proud of their first Portuguese mattress.

Mary unpacked her new sheets, blankets, and a lovely bedspread and laid them one by one on the straw mattress. Slipping some of the straw from the mattress, she used it to fill two white pillowcases, then popped them into two decorated pillowcases, and laid them at the head of the bed. When she finished, she stepped back and surveyed the finished bed nodding in approval.

Picking up Charles who was fast asleep, she laid him on the straw bed. Thoughts quickly flashed through her mind of a long-ago time in a faraway country when another mother named Mary laid her baby Son, Jesus, on a bed of hay in a manger without even a pillow for His sweet head. Mary did not complain of her lot because she had been trained to meet difficult situations graciously. She knew Mary's Son, Jesus, had slept peacefully in a stable, and now her son, Charles, already slept on their bed of straw looking so sweet and contented.

The Rentfros enjoyed their new Portuguese home. They liked to sleep with their windows open, but the landlord warned them that when thieves saw an open window, they would take a long pole with a hook on the end and fish around inside to see if they could pick up something. So, they opened their windows only a few inches.

To rest from their strenuous voyage, the Rentfros decided to spend time at the beautiful Estrela Park to enjoy the Sabbath out in nature. They returned to the park the next day to take pictures, and upon their return home, they walked out onto the veranda that overlooked the street below. Farther out they could see the blue ocean with sailing vessels dotting the horizon. Looking toward the city of Lisbon, they could see more tall buildings. In some places people jammed the narrow streets walking up and down dressed in their colorful attire.

While they were taking in the view from every direction, Mary pointed to a huge, majestic, decorated cathedral with a large cross on top. "How will we ever reach the hearts of the people who attend those churches?" she sighed. She remembered her canvassing experience trying to get in the gates in front of a cathedral. "It is so difficult to get close to those people. We are right here in the midst of the churches with crosses. Tell me, Clarence, how are we going to reach them?"

Clarence leaned against the balcony rails with his chin cupped in his two hands in deep thought. Mary's question was a serious one. How would the two of them reach the hearts of these people? He turned to Mary saying, "Mary, reaching the hearts of the people won't be easy. Heart searching will take time. This must be accompanied by fervent prayer, daily Bible study, earnest work, and planning plus plenty of patience. When we have accomplished all of this, God will step in to help us. He will show us the way to reach them."

The following day Clarence went to see Mr. Moreton of the British Bible Society in Lisbon to ask whom he could recommend as a Portuguese teacher because he and Mary were eager to begin their language studies. Mr. Moreton recommended a female teacher who gave lessons on Saturday. Clarence reached her and witnessed to her about the Sabbath and requested lessons on another day. This puzzled her, but she agreed to begin lessons with them on Friday, October 7.

Clarence knew the sooner the language was mastered, the easier it would be for them to spread the gospel. The General Conference officials advised them to take their time and learn the language very well before attempting any public speaking for the Portuguese people were a proud people and loved to hear their language spoken correctly with clear enunciation.

At their first lesson, they discovered that Portuguese was a strange language because of its nasal sounds. This made it more difficult to learn, but they persevered learning lesson after lesson.

The Rentfros still had a supply of fruits, nuts, and bread, so they were eating well. One day after their second Sabbath there, Mary gave Clarence a little money out of her small stash to go to the store to purchase a few items. After getting what he needed, he wrapped them up in a bundle, placed the bundle on his shoulder and started home. Soon he felt a tap on his back. It was the policeman again motioning for Clarence to take the bundle down. He did so and placed it under his arm. The policeman reminded him that a Portuguese gentleman must not be seen carrying bundles like a farmer. Someone might come along and spit on him or

## Chapter 31  Learning How to Live in Lisbon          135

throw eggs at him, he was told. So, Clarence reluctantly gave up his farm habits and became a gentleman as he walked toward home.

Each month Clarence filled out a report to the Iowa Conference in order to receive his allowance of money for the month. They had very little money left, and it would soon be their third week in Portugal. He worried because he had not heard a word from the Conference officials and had received nothing. Their food supply kept diminishing as the days went on. Soon they only a loaf of bread left.

He used up all his personal money that he received from selling his equipment on an installment plan. He wrote again to them, to all their friends back home, to the Iowa Conference, and to the General Conference giving them the new address hoping to receive some financial help.

> *Their food supply kept diminishing as the days went on. Soon they only a loaf of bread left.*

They heard nothing, so they rationed the loaf of bread as they continued to pray for help from the Lord. Mary got sick; then the baby became sick. Clarence felt desperate to get his allowance from the Conference. Finally, a letter from Elder Sisley in England arrived with $95 in it. Clarence had notified him of their dilemma and lack of food. Clarence decided to repay him someday for his kindness. Along with the money came a copy of *The Review and Herald*. This became food for their souls because it helped them not to feel so alienated from the denomination.

How happy Clarence felt to be able to go shopping after their long fast. As he shopped he looked for foods to help them recover. He found some unusual beans called *favas* in Portuguese. They looked so good that he chose two kilos of them. The storekeeper acted surprised to see him pick out this amount of beans, and he went outside, looked this way and that, came back in, shrugged his shoulders and began muttering as he weighed out the beans. Clarence recognized that his purchase caused some problem, but he could not figure out why.

How happy Mary felt when Clarence returned with food for her to cook. She began with the beans and soaked them overnight. The next day she placed them in a pot with water and cooked them on her little iron stove. After a few hours of cooking, she tried them, but they tasted hard. So, she cooked them for another hour. After four hours of cooking, they were still hard. "Clarence, what do you know about these beans? I can't get them to soften. Better take the rest back and ask for something else."

Clarence just abhorred taking anything back to the store. However, he knew they could not afford to throw anything away. So, off he went to the store. He handed the storekeeper a note in Portuguese asking how to eat these beans. Taking one, he demonstrated that it was hard to chew. The storekeeper did not act surprised to see Clarence return the beans and identified them as donkey beans. A donkey happened to be tied to a post outside the grocery store with a sack hanging from his neck crunching away on something. The storekeeper motioned for Clarence to follow him outside. He reached into the bag and brought up a handful of donkey beans. The men started laughing and Clarence went back to the store to select something else.

*Chapter 32*
# Starving

Clarence and Mary were diligent students spending many hours every day studying the Portuguese language. Every day they would take walks to downtown Lisbon to mingle with the people in the markets, dry goods stores, bookstores, parks, and the beach. In this way they would hear the people speaking the language, which they hoped would make it easier for them to speak it. Everywhere they walked, they took baby Charles in his stroller. Often people would comment on how the baby looked like Philippe, the crown prince of Portugal. The family became a familiar sight walking the streets of Lisbon. Many times the people would stop and talk to them in Portuguese.

They walked by fishermen's wives who cut up the fish with vigor and dexterity and filled the baskets with fish of all kinds and sizes. They discovered there were about 300 species of fish from the giant tuna to the silvery sardines and anchovies that all swim off the coast of Portugal. They also saw friendly peasant women carrying their shopping supplies and wares on their heads supported by the large *radilla* (headpiece) under the load. If the women did not carry fish baskets, they might carry large loaves of bread, heads of cabbage, laundry, or even a child. One time a woman approached them with a large clothes basket filled with vegetables upon her head. When they asked the price of turnips, she named a price twice the value, so they bargained with her to come down on the price, which she did.

However, after a few weeks, the money from Elder Sisley dwindled, and Clarence began writing letters again to try to obtain funds. He sent more letters to the Iowa Conference and to Elder Daniels at Battle Creek, Michigan. A few days later the money was gone. The family only had apples and bread to eat. Next Clarence pawned his watch and bought potatoes. They had bread and potato soup for breakfast.

After several days on this diet, they only had bread and water left to eat. Clarence pawned his precious violin and bought olive oil. They ate bread and water gravy for all three meals since they had very little food left. Mary was still nursing baby Charles and getting weak. To make matters worse, the weather became cold and rainy. Since they had no money for fuel, Clarence sawed a leg off the bed to burn in their small stove.

Day after day went by as they patiently awaited a letter from the United States with money in it to help them with their needs. Mary was anxious about the health of the baby. She was getting weak and faint on the meager diet and could not nurse. She feared they were slowly starving to death. No one knew of their plight, but she knew that God knew, and He would not forsake them. She believed God would feed them when everything else failed, but it was hard for her to deal with the delay. She wondered if the Iowa Conference really knew they were in Portugal. She cried out to Clarence saying, "Oh, Clarence, I am so hungry and weak. I feel like I am going to faint."

"God will provide for us, dear," he encouraged. He pulled his pants belt a little tighter as he, too, was so hungry. Then he took his Bible and studied Daniel 7 the rest of the day. No letter came that Sabbath. They were still eating bread and water for all three meals. They did receive some tracts from Brazil, so Clarence went out to sell them. Since it rained all day, he only found customers to buy two of the forty tracts, but he came home with two long loaves of bread even though he was soaking wet.

Every day in their family devotions they prayed hoping that some relief would come soon. The weather became colder with more rain, and the house became very damp without heat resulting in the walls dripping with moisture. The baby became sicker with a cold and other complications. Since they still had no money to purchase charcoal for heat, they became desperate and made a heart-wrenching decision to cut up the rest of their comfortable bed for fuel. They continued to saw off the legs one at a time and throw them into the iron stove. Finally, they cut off the sidebars and put the mattress on the cold floor in a corner of the bedroom.

Another two days went by. Clarence wrote notes to the Foreign Mission Board, to Jule Roberts who was treasurer of the Latin Union, and

## Chapter 32  Starving      139

to Elder Sisley in England telling them about their hunger and lack of money. Four more days passed but no help came. They received a letter from Elder Spicer without any money. A total of two months passed with no monthly salary coming. One of the biggest problems was that the people at home in the United States were not used to giving for foreign missionaries, and the treasury was empty.

Thinking that the Conference wanted them to be self-supporting, Clarence ate some bread and went out to sell papers again. He was quite weak from improper and insufficient nutrition. Baby Charles was very sick with the cold going down to his lungs accompanied by diarrhea. They had no medicine and no doctor—only a loving, weak nurse and mother who gave the baby hydrotherapy treatments night and day. The father prayed with anguished heart to God for relief. Help must come soon before it was too late.

At the end of the month, a package came from Brazil with more Portuguese tracts that Clarence ordered when they had first settled in their house. Then an answer to prayer came when Mr. Moreton lent them fifteen milreis to pay three months' rent again to the landlord. Every day when they ate their bread and water, they tried to sit at the table and thank the Lord for what they had to eat. Often Clarence would not eat his share of bread saving it for Mary and baby. The dark bread they ate was very nourishing, so they were still alive. Every day they both wept as they struggled to survive.

The rain kept coming down, and by the end of November, Clarence became so weak from hunger that he could not even get up and walk downstairs. He had no strength to go out to sell the tracts, so they had no money at all to buy any more bread. Mary was so weak that she stayed in bed because when she got up, she fell down. The bed was a warm place for her and Charles as she tried to nurse him.

On December 5 two letters came, one from Elder Sisley in England and one from Elder Starr in Iowa. They said the money was on its way to Switzerland. What happened is that the letter with the check was addressed to Clarence Rentfro, Portugal, Spain. Someone did not know that the two countries were politically separated. The Iowa Conference sent the money to the General Conference in Washington, D.C., who sent it to the Latin Union in Paris, France. There the word Spain was crossed out with the words "No Such Town. No such person here. Try Portugal and the Lisbon American Consul."

When the postman delivered the letter to the consul, he decided to take the letter to Clarence. There were tears of joy when the Rentfros received the letter the next day. That important letter contained a money order for 42,000 francs. First, they bowed in prayer thanking God for deliverance. Then Clarence drank a whole glass of hot water to help sustain him so he could walk to the bank. He made it to the bank and cashed the check.

One of the first things Clarence purchased was some fresh pineapple because they were so hungry for fresh fruit. Then, he bought an ample supply of food because he didn't know when another money order would be coming. Soon Mary and the baby began to feel better. Clarence continued his Portuguese lessons, and then he sent an order to Brazil for some more tracts, so he would have some to sell to earn money if they needed it again.

On December 9 they received ten milreis again. How thankful they felt! Clarence bought two poles and rebuilt their bed. He sent a money order to Elder Sisley to pay back the loan he received earlier. At the pawn shop, he redeemed his watch and his violin. About five days later they received letters from home, from France, books from Germany, and papers from Brazil—all in one day. This buoyed their spirits and relieved their loneliness.

Clarence started feeling better each day as he ate a balanced diet again. He gave out tracts every day like he used to do. During the three months they had been in Portugal, they reported eleven missionary visits, four Bible studies, three missionary letters, 549 tracts given out or sold and completing thirty-four days of Portuguese lessons.

*Chapter 33*
# *Busy Working for the Lord*

The Rentfros kept very busy studying the Portuguese language every day. They were eager to begin evangelistic meetings, but Elder Daniels wanted them to study diligently for two years so they could speak well enough to impress the people.

On the weekends Clarence, Mary, and baby Charles visited other churches in Lisbon, such as the Presbyterian Church, Episcopalian Church, and the United Brethren Church. It helped them with the language and acquainted them with the people in the various churches. They also visited the Art Gallery, the Botanical Gardens, and other interesting places in Lisbon.

One day while they were downtown they saw a regal procession. Don Carlos, the king of Portugal, rode past in his royal coach accompanied by the cavalry. Another time they saw him with the Emperor of Germany as they passed by in a parade.

In January 1905 Clarence received a letter from his father saying he sold a load of wheat, so he sent ten dollars as a loan. Clarence used the money to buy a Portuguese Bible to make it easier to prepare Bible studies.

One day while Mary worked around the house, she heard a knock at the door. When she opened the door, she found a pitiful woman pleading for something to eat and clothing for her naked baby. Mary felt sorry for her and gave her a loaf of bread and one of the handmade outfits that belonged to Charles. The beggar left with a smile and a nod of thanks.

Later as Clarence was walking the streets passing out tracts, he decided to go to the pawn shop to redeem his watch again because he had pawned it for expense money. As he looked around the shop, he saw an outfit just like the one baby Charles used to wear. When he went home and mentioned this to Mary, she gasped. Then she told Clarence her story about the beggar woman who used her naked baby as a decoy to obtain Mary's sympathy.

In April of 1905, Clarence decided he wanted to move out to Carcavellos about twelve miles from Lisbon. He heard that a more advanced Portuguese teacher lived there. With the help from his new teacher, they were able to obtain a very comfortable house out in the country with nearby mountains and beach. Mary loved the house and the space for a garden in the back. A cart man brought their household goods, and Clarence, Mary, and Charles traveled by train to their new location.

> *They were able to obtain a very comfortable house out in the country with nearby mountains and beach. Mary loved the house and the space for a garden in the back.*

About a week and a half later they attended the English Evangelical Church of Saint George, a church with a walled cemetery. There they met an important English lady previously married to a Portuguese actor, but now widowed. Because the Rentfros could speak English, she became friendly with them realizing how lonely they were.

The next week they organized their first Sunday School in their home. Many children attended with each participant receiving a tract. Soon after, they gave Bible studies to those interested. Besides giving studies, Mary became very busy visiting the sick and giving them treatments.

Occasionally they would travel back to Lisbon by train. One time they observed an extravagant welcome given to the king and queen of England by King Don Carlos in a parade with cavalry lancers and artillery. The streets were beautifully decorated for this reception of English nobility.

At the end of April, Clarence felt confident enough of his command of Portuguese to translate articles from English. He found a printer and began producing his own tracts. He and Mary continued to cover the area with these tracts. One day they passed out 240 of them. It became an

## Chapter 33  Busy Working for the Lord    143

unending job. Then, Clarence took on the task of translating the popular book, *Bible Readings for the Home Circle,* which took innumerable hours.

In June they found out about a campmeeting to be held in Geneva, Switzerland. Mary thought it would be a good idea for Clarence to go there, so he bought a traveling suit, packed his things, and left by train. The lengthy trip finally ended at a beautiful campground where he met other workers and gained information and encouragement. He bought some articles for Mary and Charles in Madrid and finally returned safely home to his welcoming family.

On August 9 they received a letter from Susan and Edwin Wilbur. How happy it made Mary feel to receive a letter from her sister. Even though the two sisters were separated by many thousands of miles, they enjoyed exchanging news and bringing comfort to each other. Their letters now contained their experiences in each of their respective mission countries.

Susan wrote:

When we were ready to move out among the Chinese Nationals, they did not want us to live in their villages and towns. They were afraid of foreigners. They would not even rent us a house to live in. It was very dangerous for us to go out into the interior. One time we went to visit a family, and in a short while a mob gathered around the home. The family barred all the doors and windows. The Chinese lady hid us in a back room telling us to stay there while her husband went out to try to keep the people from entering their house.

The husband slipped out of the house by a side door and met the mob out in front. While he was talking with them, Ed and I were praying to our Heavenly Father to protect His children from the angry mob. After two hours of talking the mob finally left and was not heard of again. We know that our Heavenly Father sent His angels to watch over us that night. When the lady felt that we would now be safe, she advised us to slip out quietly and quickly down a back street to reach our boat. We thanked God and the lady that night for sparing our lives from the angry mob and for taking care of us.

Every day we meet such wonderful people whom we are trying to reach with God's Word. The task is hard and rough, but we're happy to be out here among this people. We long to hear from you, Mary, as often as you can spare from your missionary duties. Take time to tell us about your adventures there in Portugal. We pray for you every day for God to give you strength and health. Be courageous, Mary, through these days of testing your faith and determination to work for the Master. This is what we both stood for. Now our reward is living for others in Christian service. Let us hear from you often.

Love, Your sister, Susan"

The letter really cheered Mary's heart. Shortly after this, Mary had a miscarriage. She stayed home and rested while Clarence continued distributing literature all over the city trying every day to make contact with the people. Sometimes he went to Lisbon to pass out tracts. One day after Mary recovered, they went to Lisbon to see one of the religious feasts to be held there. On Sunday they saw a procession of people carrying idols of saints while chanting and kneeling right in the streets. The feast continued for three days providing cultural information to the couple.

Another time the Rentfros experienced the Feast of the Saints. They saw many children dressed like beggars going from door to door begging. The children used the words, *"Pao por Deus"* which means Bread for God. To Clarence and Mary, this seemed an unusual way to take an offering.

Clarence finally received 3,000 copies of *Bible Readings for the Home Circle* that he had so diligently translated into Portuguese. Now he could pass this wonderful book to those interested in the Adventist message.

He and Mary continued to conduct the Sunday School, but Clarence decided to order songbooks so they could all sing together. He renamed the Sunday School to a Singing School. When he did this, about fifteen to thirty children and some grown-ups began to attend quite regularly to sing and to listen.

The local priest on learning of this became angry and gave orders for his members not to attend. He threatened them by saying he would not allow them to be buried in the cemetery when they died. The Rentfros discovered that the names of all the attendees were posted by the priest in the church, and the parents of the children and the others were to appear before the tribunal in the county seat. Clarence assured them that should they be forced to go to the tribunal, he would go with them. Frightened into staying away because of the threats from the priest, a few did not return, but the rest learned to sing very well accompanied by Clarence playing his violin.

One time while he held studies, Mary slipped off to go by train to Lisbon on a special shopping trip. She needed a new pair of shoes. She wore out her other shoes with all the walking she and Clarence did. She successfully purchased a pair which was her first new pair since arriving in the mission field.

*Chapter 34*
# *Working in Carcavellos*

The people of Lisbon and Carcavellos became accustomed to seeing Mary appear in her white nurse's uniform about the streets and churches. They soon learned that she was a kind nurse who would come to their homes to help treat their sick family members. They began to call her "Doña Mary." When a doctor was called it would usually take him five or six days before he could make the visit. Mary would be called upon to deliver babies, sometimes as many as five a week. She also nursed the sick with water treatments and other natural healing remedies. One time she visited a sick baby who later died. She felt so sad about it even though she had done all she could to save it. She had called the doctor for more help, but he told her he could not come for a week.

At times she received calls to neighboring villages to give treatments to sick families. She felt she was witnessing for her Saviour every time she went to these homes. She became known as the "angel of mercy" as she went about doing the best she could for her Master. He blessed her nursing ability and gave her words to speak to the sick ones and their loved ones.

A place that the Rentfros visited in Cascais lay out in the ocean by a huge rock. It still exists and actually looks like a very large hole with a red lining like a whale's mouth. The sea flows into the deep bottom of the chasm and slams against the rocky walls. Visitors rush down to see

## Chapter 34  Working in Carcavellos        147

the inside when the tide goes out. However, this becomes extremely dangerous when the tide rolls in with its crashing waves. This place is called "Boca do Inferno," or Hell's Mouth, because when ships drift into it, they are shipwrecked.[5]

One night Clarence heard a wailing sound coming from a ship in distress. Its SOS called all able men to rush out to help them. He hurriedly dressed and ran down to the beach to the chasm to see what he could do to help. He arrived in time to throw out the lifeline to a man who began swimming with all his might toward the stricken vessel. More men arrived bringing huge baskets which were tied onto a strong, thick rope. When the man with the first part of the rope reached the ship, someone on deck dropped a strong rope. These two ends were tied together tightly. The man on deck pulled the rope up and strung it through an iron ring on deck. Then he dropped it back to the man in the water who took it back to shore to get the baskets. Unloading the passengers into the baskets one by one continued. Back and forth the men drew the baskets from boat to shore and back again bringing passengers to safety.

Clarence began singing "Throw out the Lifeline" as they worked. When they finished and everyone evacuated the boat, Clarence and the other men went home. By morning the boat had disappeared in Boca do Inferno.

The Rentfros continued to conduct Sunday Schools and Singing Schools, but on February 3, 1906, they began their first official Sabbath School with the three Rentfros attending. The following week Clarence purchased some Portuguese Bibles in anticipation of the new members who would soon be attending. As more people became interested in the Adventist message, the Rentfros felt the need for an assistant.

Then, they heard from Elder W. A. Spicer telling them that he would stop to see them on his way to Africa. When he arrived Clarence hired a carriage to drive Elder Spicer all over Lisbon, Carcavellos, and the villas to show him the vast territory, the people, the customs, all the beautiful cathedrals with the huge crosses upon them, and the saints on the street with containers to receive offerings from the people. Elder Spicer seemed duly impressed with the sights and the vast mission field.

Elder Spicer commended Mary and Clarence for the excellent work of distributing so many tracts, and he took note of all those interested in the Adventist truth. Before he left, he praised Clarence for translating *Bible Readings for the Home Circle* into Portuguese and having it printed in small volumes.

Clarence wanted charts to illustrate his sermons, so he purchased unbleached cloth from a local factory. He made a Ten Commandments

---
5    http://1ref.us/r8. Accessed 12/10/18.

chart to hang on the wall in the room where they held Sabbath School. Later he made his own prophetic charts.

After all the months of diligent, faithful study and mingling with the Portuguese people, Clarence had learned the language so well that he now could preach his first sermon in Portuguese to people in the first public meeting in a rented hall on April 17, 1906. In his first sermon, he discussed the state of the dead. The Portuguese people who attended that meeting were of the upper class of Lisbon. Since Clarence advertised he would discuss the dead, the people dressed in black. The ladies wore black hats, gloves, shoes, and dresses while the men wore black suits with black gloves and carried canes hooked over their arms.

The seats in the meeting room were all taken, and the hallways were filled with standing room only. Mary and Clarence felt amazed and so happy that God blessed their work. What a day of rejoicing for the couple, for on that day the Seventh-day Adventist work was officially launched in Portugal.

In June of 1906, Elder Spicer responded to the plea for help from Clarence, and another pastor arrived in Portugal. Ernesto Schwantes with his wife and son came to Lisbon and stayed a short time with the Rentfros before being assigned to O'Porto. While the family stayed with the Rentfros, their son, Arnold, distributed 1,840 tracts which greatly helped Clarence and Mary in their work. Elder Schwantes believed in colporteur work and began widely distributing literature in O'Porto with the help of Antonio Figueiredo, a young man interested in the Adventist truth.

One of the first converts to Adventism happened to be Mrs. Lucy Portugal, the woman they met at the English Evangelical Church of St. George who spoke English and became friendly with the Rentfros. Because of her friendliness, they sent her the magazine, *Signs of the Times*, and after several months they went to visit her. She lived in a beautiful home, and a maid opened the door when they visited. Clarence gave her his card, and the maid placed it on a silver tray, then took it to Mrs. Portugal. The maid returned with permission for them to enter.

The Rentfros followed the maid to the main living room and sat down. Clarence noticed an open Bible on the table with a copy of the *Signs of the Times* emphasizing the Sabbath. When Mrs. Portugal entered the room, he asked her if she enjoyed the paper.

"Oh, yes," she replied enthusiastically. "I have found the true Sabbath by reading this paper. I have my mind fully made up to keep the Sabbath of the Lord. However, I must first speak to a minister about this strange day."

## Chapter 34  Working in Carcavellos    149

Right then Clarence invited her to attend Sabbath School, and she happily accepted the invitation. However, since she lived twelve miles away from the Rentfros, she asked if they could come to her home. The following Sabbath, they organized a Sabbath School at her home at Rua dos Industriais #9 with three adults and baby Charles in attendance.

While Clarence busied himself with passing out tracts, Mary became very busy in 1905 and 1906 with her nursing. People began sending for her as they had for a doctor. She did her best to treat the sick with natural remedies she had learned about in Iowa. She became creative in choosing treatments for the people because there were no antibiotics or medicines available. Also, there were few doctors in the area, and it took days before one came to see patients. Unlike the doctors, Mary did not charge for her services.

*Chapter 35*

# Back to Lisbon

In August of 1906 the lease was up on their home in Carcavellos, so they moved back to Lisbon at Rua de Sao Bernardo #120. The house was large enough so they could live there and continue the Singing School. Clarence translated songs into Portuguese, taught them to the people that came to sing, and played his violin to accompany them. At the end of the month, seven people attended Sabbath School.

Doctors were scarce in Portugal, and if one could be found, he usually was busy. Since Mary received training in childbirth when she worked at the Iowa Sanitarium in Des Moines and because of her experience in Portugal as a midwife, she decided to deliver her own daughter. So, she proceeded to instruct Clarence to be her assistant. When it came time for delivery on August 27, 1906, she and Clarence followed the proper procedures. As the baby emerged, they had some difficulty getting the baby to breathe, and she gasped for air.

## Chapter 35  Back to Lisbon

Mary cried out to Jesus, "Oh, please don't let my baby daughter die. She will be our merry sunshine here."

Jesus answered her heartfelt prayer, and baby Marian started breathing normally. Marian became the first Seventh-day Adventist missionary baby born in Portugal. The couple discovered that children born in the city of Lisbon are called "alfacinhas," or lettuce-eaters, because of the abundance of lettuce grown in that area. To be called a lettuce-eater made Marian feel proud as she grew older.

After two years of faithful work searching for hungry souls, Mary and Clarence rejoiced with tears to see their first fruits of labor baptized in the turbulent waves of the Atlantic Ocean at the mouth of a small river. The baptism occurred on September 21, 1906, on a dark night, with only the faint light of the twinkling stars shining down on the four candidates baptized by Elder Ernesto Schwantes. The night baptism protected the candidates, which included a minor, from interference by the Catholic authorities.

Among the candidates was Mrs. Portugal. As a refined English lady, and as a friend to the Rentfros, she helped them with her knowledge of three languages, French, English, and Portuguese. Her contacts with people who spoke these languages interested others in the church. She became secretary and treasurer of the church and held these offices for many years. Being a friend, helper, guide, and counselor to the Rentfros made her valuable to the advancement of the Adventist Church. As the first convert, her name became a historical symbol of the beginning of Seventh-day Adventism in Portugal. Charles and his siblings-to-come would grow to admire Mrs. Portugal and would think it amazing that she bore the name of the adopted country of their parents.

In November Mary experienced something unusual. As she worked around the house, she heard a knock at the door. There stood a coachman attired in all the finery of royalty with a beautiful carriage drawn by white horses with decorated harnesses parked on the sidewalk in front of the house. Mary's eyes widened with surprise. The coachman handed her a written invitation for Doutora Doña Maria. It read as follows:

Excellencia Doña Maria, Doutora,

Please come with this coachman to the palace of the Marquis of Pombal of the Royal House of Portugal. My wife is very sick. We will be honored with your presence. Muitas graças.

Senhor Marquez de Pombal, Royal Palace, Lisbon

The coachman said he would wait for Doña Maria in the coach. Mary hurried upstairs to put on her uniform and to tell Clarence. Clarence dressed baby Charles while Mary dressed. Before leaving, the Rentfros asked God's guidance and blessing as they were about to meet some of the members of the Royal House of Portugal. They hurried downstairs and joined the coachman in the carriage. How special they felt in the coach as the horses trotted through the streets and arrived on the palace grounds. Palace workers guided the Rentfros through the glimmering hallways and apartments until they reached the apartment where the marquis' wife lay in distress. Clarence and the baby waited outside the area while Mary treated the woman bringing her much-needed relief.

After Mary completed treatment, she received heartfelt, grateful "thank yous" from the marquis as she and her family followed her out to the waiting coach.

Mary could hardly wait to discuss this experience with Clarence until they reached home. When they arrived and thanked the coachman for the transportation, Mary could not stop talking about all the things she saw and did at the palace. They also thanked God for His help and asked that He would continue to help them if any future requests came from the palace.

They often left by coach to assist in the health problems of the royal family during the time they were in Lisbon. One patient Mary worked with for some time was an English lady, wife of the royal coachman. As the Duchess of Fial, she held a doctor's degree as a veterinarian and worked with horse training. She also was a cousin to Queen Maria of Portugal.

With her expertise as a midwife, Mary delivered all the babies born in the palace and with other royalty at that time. In all it is estimated that she had delivered about 1,000 babies during the time they lived in Portugal. Through the following years as the Rentfros increased their family, their children often rode in the royal coach, played in the royal gardens, received treats from the royal family, and enjoyed privileges other children did not have.

When the children grew up they each had pleasant memories of visiting the palace. Young Charles often experienced extra rides in the coach to keep him happy while Mary worked inside the palace delivering babies or treating the sick. Their daughter remembers being pushed in a swing by the crown prince, and the youngest son became fascinated with the wheels of the palace carriages and remembered them all his life.

*Chapter 36*
# *Becoming a Leader*

In the Sabbath School meeting room of their home, services were held every Wednesday and Sabbath for several years. Cheap furniture, a crude rostrum for the pulpit covered with dark cloth, and a small portable organ made the room suitable for meetings. The Portuguese people were used to seeing images and statues in their churches, but when they entered the Adventist meeting place, they saw charts on the wall made of white muslin with drawings of large animals from Daniel and the Revelation plus a list of the Ten Commandments.

When interested newcomers came to the advertised meetings, they walked up to the front, knelt before Clarence, made the sign of the cross, and returned to find a seat. It took time, but the Rentfros helped the people to understand that these rituals were not necessary. They knew the people were not heathen but just lacked the true knowledge of a living Saviour. By October, fifteen people attended their Sabbath School.

The Rentfros often visited other churches, even Catholic ones. They took time to visit the convent of Jerónimos and many other cathedrals with their fascinating historical backgrounds. In the catacombs under the huge cathedrals, they saw all types of devices for torturing Christians because of their faith during the period of the Inquisition. They also visited churches where the bodies of former kings of Portugal were buried.

Another baptism held on December 6, 1906, included some members of the Figueiredo family. With the membership of the church increasing, at the beginning of the new year, Clarence decided to buy a dozen more chairs. He also received the gift of an organ from Adventist church members in Colorado, California, Nebraska, and Iowa who raised money for it. Larger than his current organ, it had pedals and a larger pump. How exciting to have the capacity to make more beautiful music for their church! Clarence even taught young Charles to play the organ so he could assist in the meetings.

Clarence received another unexpected gift—$50, so he decided to buy a pair of shoes since his three-year-old shoes were worn through from all the walking he did to pass out tracts day after day. Before buying shoes at the sapataria, a place where shoes are made to order, Clarence asked about the various types of shoes. When the man took his foot measurements, he asked if Clarence spoke English. The shoe clerk wanted to find an English tutor for his son, Alberto.

"I'd be happy to teach him if he could come to my home," Clarence offered. This request excited him because he saw it as an opportunity to witness for Christ. He and the clerk arranged a time and day for the lessons.

Alberto came faithfully for his English lessons at the Rentfros' home for weeks. A firm friendship developed between him and the Rentfro family. He also began absorbing some of the spiritual atmosphere of the home causing his father to decide to send his son to England for further study. His father viewed the Adventist faith as a strange religion and wanted to get Alberto away from its influence. However, he also wanted him to speak good English so he would have a future and be able to earn a good living.

When Alberto settled with a family in England, he discovered that their neighbor was a Bible instructor from America. She used to live in Iowa and happened to know the Rentfros. Alberto received an invitation to attend Bible studies in her home which he gladly accepted because of his friendship with the Rentfros in Portugal. Soon he became a baptized member of the Seventh-day Adventist Church in England.

When he turned eighteen years old, his father sent for him to come home. Alberto knew that his father expected him to learn the shoe-making profession and advance in that career. Alberto did not want to be a shoemaker, so at first, he resisted his father's call, but he had a terrible dream that if he did not return to Portugal, his family would be lost. So, he returned to Portugal and went directly to the Rentfros home. He asked Clarence to go with him to his house to try to explain to his father that he did not want to become a shoemaker. Clarence agreed to go, and they left right away. Alberto's father opened the door when they knocked, and he acted overwhelmed with joy to see Alberto as well as Clarence.

"Come in, come in," he beckoned to them.

After visiting for a few minutes, Alberto announced, "Father, I'm happy to see you and to be home, but I want you to know that I do not want to be a shoemaker. Since I found Jesus as my Saviour and have been baptized, I want to serve Him and work for the church that showed me the truth as it is in the Bible."

"Oh, no!" exclaimed the man as his dreams for his son shattered in a matter of seconds.

"Please, Son, give up this strange religion. It will only bring you harm."

"I cannot!" Alberto answered in a determined voice.

"Then, I will kill myself," declared his father as he clasped his hands to his chest as if his son had ripped out his heart.

His mother hearing her husband's threats rushed into the room and soon understood what was happening. "Please, Son," she pleaded as she fell on her knees before Alberto. "Give up these foolish ideas, and follow your father's plan for your life."

Alberto repeated his answer, "I cannot." She could see the determination in the tightness of his lips. He continued, "Mother, I must obey God."

Then, his father seeing how firm his son felt about obeying and serving God, yielded to him and decided to hire him temporarily in his own store. For two years until he turned twenty years old, Alberto served faithfully in his father's store.

His father then contacted Clarence asking, "What do you have in mind for my son's education?"

Clarence readily responded by saying, "I think he should go to Gland, Switzerland, to learn French and study business at our school there."

Alberto did go to school in Switzerland and studied business. When he returned to Portugal in 1914, he felt called to become an evangelist. His mother and sister were baptized without the knowledge of Alberto's father, which angered him so much when he found out that he would not allow them to attend church for two years. Finally, they did attend, and Alberto went on to become the secretary and treasurer of the Portuguese Mission where he served for a while. Next, he established a church in Cabo Verde, became a pastor, then a teacher in the Seminary in Porto Alegre. After a few more years, he returned to Lisbon and became secretary and treasurer there until he retired. In 1966 he became ill with leukemia and died leaving a long legacy of service to the church he loved as a young man.

Clarence learned that campmeeting would soon be held in Switzerland, and he wanted his family to attend with him this time. So, they packed up their things and headed out on the train to Badajoz where they met another train to Seville, Spain, then on to Valencia where they stayed overnight with Frank Bond, one of the two brothers who was chosen to be the first missionaries in Spain, the country that Clarence longed to evangelize. They held no envious feelings toward Frank Bond and enjoyed attending one of his meetings to see the results of the work there. Traveling on, the Rentfros went to Barcelona and stayed with Walter Bond, the other brother, and his family. Walter Bond invited Clarence to preach there for several meetings before the Rentfros traveled on to Gland, Switzerland, and the campmeeting where they heard Elder Prescott preach.

May 25, 1907, became a day of rejoicing for Clarence and Mary at campmeeting, a day for which they prayed, hoped, and diligently worked ever since Clarence began his canvassing and ministerial work in 1900 in the Iowa Conference. Clarence and three other young men experienced an ordination ceremony. Walter and Frank Bond were also ordained along with Clarence. Elder A. G. Daniels, president of the General Conference, administered the charge to the young pastors and discussed their responsibilities of ministering to others. After the ordination prayer, Clarence became an official pastor in the Seventh-day Adventist Church. Everyone welcomed these new pastors into the ministerial group attending the campmeeting.

*Chapter 37*
# New Converts

How happy the Rentfros felt as they traveled home to Portugal from the Switzerland campmeeting! As an ordained minister, Clarence could now lead out in all the functions of the church. His official title now would be superintendent of the Portuguese Mission. Among other things, his duties included sending in a report to the Latin Union each month with a list of his expenditures and needs to build up the work in that area.

Their local work seemed to be progressing quite well. Clarence introduced freewill offering to the church group, and the people responded gladly because they gave in their former churches. By passing out tracts, along with reaching out to nearby villages,

> *Clarence and Mary gave tracts to the bread man, milkman, vegetable and fruit man, and anyone they saw.*

and presenting Bible studies to interested people, the Rentfros experienced results in baptisms. Clarence and Mary gave tracts to the bread man, milkman, vegetable and fruit man, and anyone they saw. The tracts were having a positive effect throughout Portugal because people often came to them wanting explanations about various religious subjects.

They also began using the newspapers to promote the church. A reporter from the newspaper, *O Século Ilustrado*, or *The Illustrated Cen-*

*tury*, interviewed Clarence and took a picture of him standing in the pulpit with a prophetic chart on the wall behind him. The article declared that the method Clarence consistently used included the printed charts. Many readers became curious about the charts and contacted the Rentfros.

The Rentfros discovered that in the best interest of the church it was a good idea to move their meetings to various locations around Lisbon in order to contact different groups of people. Using their home as a setting for meetings saved extra meeting hall rentals. So, after their first home location brought in new people resulting in Bible studies, they moved to a new location. One time they moved just down the street above a store, and another time they moved to a place near a cable car route. When the noisy cable cars came clanking and clattering by, it became very disturbing to the listeners, so the Rentfro family moved again.

Clarence described this and other city noises in one of his own writings. "The cable runs from about seven o'clock one morning to about one o'clock the next morning. The noise disturbs our rest at night, and is hard on the nerves. About three o'clock every morning come the street cleaners with brooms, shovels, and carts or machine sweepers. At four o'clock pass the carts hauling vegetables to market to be sold to retailers. About five o'clock come the retailers with their pack burros to buy their supply for selling from house to house or pass the women with wooden-soled shoes which are secured only over the toes, the heels going 'clack, clack, clack' over the stone walks. By six o'clock the sellers are on their return with produce to sell. And what a noise comes from the throats of persons of both sexes of all ages from wee children to old men and women! The cries come from lungs trained and untrained, from husky groans to clear, ringing voices; some with a singing voice, others with a wild scream. A few really make out a tune, either in a minor or major key, mostly minor."[6]

One evening during song service as Clarence played the organ, the church members sang in extra melodious tones. A white man and his young black son entered the hall, sat near the back, and listened attentively to the singing. As the meeting progressed, they became more interested in the service and the sermon. At the close of the meeting, Clarence went to the back to meet them. The man told Clarence his name was José de Oliveria, and he and his son, Artur, were Catholics on a vacation from Angola, Africa. As they were walking past the meeting place, they heard the beautiful singing. Curiosity drew them inside, so Clarence invited them to continue attending the meetings. During the following days, the man came to Bible studies and shared his new

---

6   Rentfro, Clarence K. "Worldwide Field—Portugal." *Advent Review and Sabbath Herald*. July 23, 1908. p. 12.

## Chapter 37  New Converts

truths with his son and his niece. As his friendship with the Rentfros grew, Jose decided to be baptized along with Artur and his niece.

José owned a large soap factory with forty employees, and the first Friday evening after he returned to Angola, he shut down the factory and invited his employees and their families to attend Sabbath School and church the next day. He continued to hold services and to send the tithes and offerings he collected to Clarence who sent them on to the Latin Union. As José's group grew in attendance, Clarence requested a worker to help Jose.

Elder Nance Anderson soon arrived in Angola where he baptized a large group of people. José was ordained as an elder while his niece became secretary-treasurer of the new company there. Artur grew up and lived among his relatives there.

A young mother, Elvira Barreiros, along with her twelve-year-old daughter, Judith, were attending Protestant meetings elsewhere when their neighbor told them about meetings held by the Rentfros. They were interested in finding out about this new religion, so one evening they walked into a meeting. Impressed by the simplicity of the place, the dress of the members, and Mary's gracious welcome as they entered, Elvira kept her ears and eyes open. The charts on the walls pricked her curiosity. After their first visit, they came back from time to time and eventually became members. Later Mr. Barreiros was baptized, too.

The Rentfros invited Judith to come to their home during the summer. She enjoyed helping Mary with the housework and playing with the children. Clarence taught her to play the organ, and with practice, she soon played hymns for the meetings. One evening her mother, Elvira, presented the subject of the Sabbath and called on Judith to stand up and repeat the Ten Commandments. After her perfect recitation of them, her mother asked, "Is it difficult for you to keep the Sabbath?"

Shyly at first, Judith responded by saying, "It is hard when I go to school. The other students often call me names and play tricks on me. My friends don't talk to me anymore, so I feel lonely most of the time."

Like a caring family, the congregation became very supportive of Judith. Many listeners gave her hugs after the service. Others promised to pray for her.

During her stay with the Rentfros, Mary taught Judith how to sew and make garments for babies. She also learned how Mary assisted in the birth of twins born to a neighbor. All these things helped Judith to grow into a fine young woman.

*Chapter 38*

# The Revolution

    On February 2, 1908, a tragedy occurred in Lisbon because some revolutionists in the city did not like the union of church and state. So, after the royal family returned from England, riding in an open carriage, they made their way from the docks to the palace. Prince Manuel rode horseback just ahead of the carriage in the procession. Several of the revolutionists rushed up to the carriage, and quick as a flash jumped up beside the king and shot him in the face killing him instantly and then killed Dom Louis Felipe, traveling with the family. The queen mother, Doña Amelia, kept waving her bouquet of roses in front of the assassin trying to divert his attention until the guards reached their carriage. Prince Manuel received a shot in his arm wounding him severely but not killing him. He recovered and became king taking his father's place.

    When the Rentfros heard of these terrible events, they felt very sad because of their previous personal connection with the royal family. They decided to retreat to their country home in Caxias away from the revolution chaos. This home at Calcado de Laveiras #131 was a favorite of the family because it was located on a peaceful two-acre lot with room for the children to play. Surrounded by a thick high stone wall, the two-story house afforded privacy and some protection from the dirt road out in front. Living near the hills and beaches, the family could take a hike into the hills or take a lunch down to the beach and play in the water as the occasion arose.

## Chapter 38  The Revolution

Every morning bright and early a shepherd boy passed by driving a flock of sheep on to greener pastures in the surrounding hills. A little later in the morning, the family could see the green hills covered with what looked like white powder puffs. These white puffs were the gentle sheep grazing lazily with playful lambs nibbling here and there scampering about. The shepherd boy stopped by the Rentfros home every day and picked up their nanny goat with its kid and took them to the verdant hills for the day returning them around sunset time.

Although the Rentfros lived in a safe, quiet place, most of Portugal erupted in turmoil and unrest because of the assassinations. Clarence attended the funeral of the fallen king and Dom Louis Felipe along with many soldiers and representatives of other nations. As the country mourned for its leader, many of the Portuguese people appeared to be stressed and confused. This sad state continued for several years.

Prince Manuel at nineteen years of age, became king of Portugal in 1908. During his short reign, he tried to set up a representative government, but he was too young to hold the kingdom together. Internal political strife brought on a period of national weakness and instability. Protestantism seemed to be growing, but the hierarchy of the Catholic Church opposed it because under the monarchy they enjoyed a comfortable union of the church with the state. A group calling themselves Republicans adopted an anti-religious policy. Converts and churches were attacked, while clergy and their followers suffered persecution.

Due to the unrest and chaos, social services for the poor were neglected. Once while Clarence was doing missionary work in O'Porto he found a young fourteen-year-old orphan boy living with an uncle. Clarence contacted Mary telling her that the boy needed a home and asked permission to bring him to their home. Mary approved, so Joao do Sa came to live with them. He enjoyed being with the Rentfros and helped Mary with the house chores and with the garden. He ran errands, delivered announcements for the meetings, and sold Portuguese Bibles and books that Clarence translated. The Rentfros praised his hard work and enjoyed his pleasant personality.

When Joao became old enough, he served his required time in the army, but after being discharged, he returned to help the Rentfros with the meetings. Clarence and Mary decided he should go to Gland, Switzerland, to study in our schools there. After studying hard he graduated from the nurses' course and ministerial training. When he returned to Portugal, he worked canvassing in O'Porto. Next, he preached in Porto Alegre and later went as a missionary to Angola in Africa.

While living in their country home in Caixias, Mary, with Clarence assisting her, delivered a little brother for Charles and Marian on April 30, 1909, named Curtis Stanford Rentfro. Big brother, Charles, remembers trying to go into his parents' bedroom the day he was born, but the door was locked. He pulled a chair over to the keyhole and tried to peek in because he heard a baby cry. After a while, Clarence introduced him to his new little brother.

Since Curtis arrived prematurely, the parents needed to incubate him. They coated him with olive oil and wrapped him in cotton batting. At night Clarence held him on his warm chest securely wrapped in a blanket. During the day they placed him in a shoebox and put it in the unlit wood stove which was warm after its use at night. He survived and became an active little fellow. However, he could not stand cold water because it would make his fingernails and lips turn blue.

Even though their family enlarged, Clarence kept on in his pursuit of knowledge while Mary kept on nursing the poor. Clarence decided he should learn Greek, so he began taking lessons. Some days as he studied, the children would climb up onto his lap. Besides Charles and Marian, Curtis was old enough to be part of the lap climbers at that time. Clarence just kept studying as he rocked the children to sleep. Other times as he studied, they would crawl all over him or tug at his arms for attention. He never pushed them aside, but just kept studying.

*Chapter 39*

# Trying Times

In August Clarence traveled to the campmeeting in Switzerland to give his annual report to the assembly of the Latin Union telling of the progress of the Adventist work in Portugal. Part of his speech follows:

"During the last two years we have held meetings in the two principal cities of Lisbon and O'Porto. Meetings were held four times a week including Sabbath. Three people were baptized in January, three in June, and others will be baptized soon. Two colporteurs are selling books. We enjoyed religious freedom for a while in Portugal, so we made use of this privilege by scattering the seed of truth. Sister White said that the printed page should be scattered like the leaves of autumn."

> *Three people were baptized in January, three in June, and others will be baptized soon.*

This is just what Clarence and Mary did day by day. They scattered papers and tracts to everyone. In spite of this modest way of spreading the message, the Advent movement progressed in Lisbon because of God's blessing.

During the revolution years from 1908 to 1910, the trains stopped running as did all other transportation. Clarence walked from their home in Caixas to Lisbon to inquire about the safety of the Adventist Church members. Since soldiers shot bullets to scare the revolutionists, many times Clarence dodged some of those bullets as he walked along.

The fighting raged between two factions near a certain spot where a small river emptied into the Atlantic Ocean. Clarence needed to cross over the river bridge, but it was too dangerous. So he chose a spot by the railroad bridge and dropped down below it. Clinging to the edge of the bridge, he passed one hand over the other on the ties attempting to cross over to the other side where small fishing boats docked in the water. However, as he neared the opposite shore, his hands slipped, and he landed in the water soaking his good suit. Catching the edge of one of the boats, he climbed aboard, reached up for one of the ties and continued crossing under the bridge. He waited at the end of the bridge until the sound of whizzing bullets stopped. With a prayer of thanks for his deliverance, he proceeded on to Lisbon, his suit drying on the way.

During this time of great unrest, the police feared revolts against the government, so they required religious groups to obtain a permit to hold public meetings. Fanatical groups roamed the streets going from one Protestant church to another causing disturbances and agitating the people with their boisterous manner making trouble for the police. The Rentfros read in the newspaper how these men would enter the churches and break up the services by their loud, disorderly ways showing no reverence. Some rioters would go into the churches and beat up the people there while robbing them of their valuables.

Then, they would break up the furniture, plunder the offices, and even kill those who try to stop them. Because of the havoc caused by the revolution, some church groups were unable to meet together at all.

When the trains resumed their schedules, Clarence revived his evangelistic meetings in Lisbon with the help of an assistant. The Latin Union sent Paul Meyer from Switzerland who would also help with the work in O'Porto. Clarence moved his meetings once again; this time to a hall on the second floor of an apartment building at Rua das Chagas #9A. Because unruly groups still persecuted the various churches, Clarence hoped and prayed that the Lisbon meetings would be safe from the fanatical instigators.

One Sunday evening people began entering the meeting place while Mary stood at the door greeting them and handing out songbooks. Clarence played hymns on the organ, and Paul Meyer led the singing. A few of the church members attended the meeting that night along with interested visitors totaling about forty people. Most people were seated when sixteen

## Chapter 39  Trying Times

young men came up the stairs and entered the room. The young men greeted Mary pleasantly, and she showed them to some empty seats scattered among the people already seated. Clarence and Paul also noticed the newcomers, but the group joined in the singing, and nothing unusual happened. Mary knew how other churches were disturbed by angry ruffians of an anti-religious sect, and she felt rather suspicious of so many young men entering their meeting together. Praying silently to God, she trusted His protection. She knew God could rescue them if needed, and she asked for His special help that evening.

After the song service, Paul invited the congregation to kneel for prayer, but the young men did not kneel. Mary tried not to anticipate trouble, but when she saw the young men give each other smirky smiles, she worried there would be problems. She continued to pray silently for God's help and wisdom to know what to do if a riot occurred. She also prayed for protection for the furniture, organ, songbooks, and the things they had purchased through much sacrifice.

After the prayer Clarence began the sermon, and Mary signaled to Paul to come to the back of the room. They stepped out into the hall to confer about what would be the best way to handle the situation in case things got out of control. Mary asked Paul to remain in the back with her so they could be ready for action.

Nothing happened as Clarence preached, but he, too, noticed the young men with cynical looks on their faces. As they looked around the room at the large charts with strange-looking beasts on them, they pretended to be interested in the sermon for a while. As the hour slowly slipped away, and just at the highest point of interest, the ringleader could contain himself no longer. He gave a signal, and all the young men jumped up from their seats shouting, then began pulling down the charts and hitting people.

Mrs. Portugal quickly took the children out of the room by a side door and up to the third floor, closing the door tightly for safety. Clarence and Paul both tried to stop the disturbance, but to no avail. Clarence moved to the organ and began playing and singing hymns hoping to quiet the intruders, but no one listened to the music. One of the church members slipped out in the confusion and ran to a nearby police station for help.

The unruly lunatics were hitting people, knocking over chairs, shoving, and slamming people all about. Mary tried to talk with them, but they showed no respect to her. Mary was a petite woman, quick, agile, and full of energy. Her big brown eyes snapped when she saw the ringleader knock a white-haired church member down on the floor. She still had her hat on and remembered the large hat pin that she always used to hold her hat in place.

*I wonder if I could use it as a weapon*, she thought.

Quick as a flash she pulled the long shiny pin out of her hat with her right hand. She stepped over to the ringleader who was beating the poor old man on the floor. With her left hand, she grabbed the ruffian by his hair, jerked back his head, and showed him the sharp gleaming hatpin aimed toward his skull. The ruffian immediately stopped hitting the old man who was gasping for breath on the floor. The rioter threw up his arms in fear as he stared at the sharp steel hatpin. "Get up off that man!" Mary ordered.

She kept the hatpin aimed at him as he rushed for the door crying, "My God, let me out of here." Mary stayed behind him with the long, shiny, steel hatpin pointed at his back.

As she was forcing him toward the rear door and stairway, she motioned to Paul who was a strong, six-foot-tall man. Paul suddenly grabbed the ruffian, swung the door wide and gave him a good swift kick down the stairs, and he went tumbling head over heels right into the arms of the police who had just arrived. As the police handcuffed him, the rioter bit the hand of the policeman, which did not help matters.

"That leaves fifteen," Mary commented to Paul and went after another young ruffian. With the loss of their ringleader, the other ruffians did not resist much as they were escorted to the door and kicked down the stairs by Paul. All the police needed to do was to pick up the men as they came tumbling down the stairs. This was one of the easiest arrests the police had done at church meetings. These young men never anticipated all the trouble they would have when they entered that religious meeting.

Soon Mary heard the shrill whistle of the police and the rumbling of the police wagon wheels rolling over the cobblestones. Opening one of the windows, she listened for the rumbling sound to end as it moved into the distance. Then, she turned to Clarence who was still playing the organ and announced that the rioters were gone. They enjoyed a moment of peace as the remaining people returned to their seats. After a quiet prayer of thanks to the Heavenly Father for watching over them, Clarence closed the meeting. Mary checked with each member to see if any of their injuries needed treatment, but they all escaped serious problems and went safely to their homes.

The next morning a policeman came to the Rentfros with a written message from the chief to come to the police station to press charges against the rioters. Clarence went to sign the complaint. Because the ringleader had bitten a policeman's finger, he received a sentence of one-year imprisonment, but Clarence requested leniency, and his sentence became six months instead. The other fifteen young men received a good scolding from the chief of police and turned loose. They never returned to bother the Rentfros and their meetings.

For years after this experience, Clarence hired the protection of the friendly police to keep order during his meetings. The country of Portugal continued to struggle to guarantee their new rights of civil and religious freedom in a land which for thousands of years had been Catholic to the core as well as a bulwark of the Inquisition stronghold in southern Europe.

As more fighting continued, Clarence thought of a plan. He bought many yards of red, white, and blue bunting at the local store and made a pattern for Charles to use in cutting out stars while Mary with her skillful fingers, just like Betsy Ross, fashioned a large United States flag during the night. The next morning, he hung it out the second floor window. Bullets whizzed about, and it was not safe to be out in the streets, but the breeze gently unfurled the star-spangled, striped flag from its long pole, and it waved back and forth for the rebels to see as they rushed about. No one bothered the Rentfros in the apartment above the meeting place with the American flag snapping in the wind.

*Chapter 40*

# *Family Experiences*

One evening during this time period, a large bright light lit up the sky so brilliantly one evening that the people were startled and frightened. Some ran outside screaming and pleading for the Lord to save them from imminent destruction. They called on their favorite saints, and many came to the Rentfros asking for help in their distress for they believed the world was ending. The Rentfros went outside and discovered the most beautiful sight they had ever seen. Halley's Comet was passing over Portugal and would not return for seventy-five years.

The people calmed down after understanding this phenomenon, and Mary and Clarence continued with the evening meetings which for the most part were pleasant, but not all of them. One night a man wearing an overcoat appeared to be friendly and milled about in the congregation after the meeting. He saw Clarence's violin and wanted it. He moved closer to it as it lay in a chair near the front of the room. When he thought no one saw him, he quickly and quietly picked up the violin, placed it under his overcoat, and walked out of the meeting into the darkness outside.

No one missed the violin until everyone had left and Mary asked, "Where is your violin, Clarence?"

Clarence immediately moved to the front and looked at the chair where he had laid it. "It was right here, but now it's gone."

How shocked he felt when he saw the empty chair! Mary felt sad over the loss of the precious instrument. Clarence had played it at every meeting in Portugal as well as playing it in the Iowa evangelistic meetings. How could they ever replace it?

One of the men who attended the meetings at that location heard about the loss of the violin and realized it would hinder the effect of the evangelistic meetings. This man made violins as a profession. One evening he came to the meetings earlier than usual with a strange package under his arm. Seeing Clarence near the front of the room, he walked over to him and presented a special violin made just for him. Surprised and touched, Clarence pressed it to his heart and expressed his deep thanks. Then, he tenderly lifted it into position under his chin, took the bow, ran it across the strings, closed his eyes, and enjoyed the melodious sound as he played a hymn that filled the empty room with its sweet resonance. The new violin was used in many meetings and evangelistic efforts in Portugal, Brazil, South America, and in the United States. It is currently a keepsake in the Rentfro family.

When Mary was not busy helping Clarence at the meetings, she worked at making all the family's clothing on an old Wheeler and Wilson sewing machine. However, as time went on, the machine began having problems. The thread broke, then the stitches jumped. It stuck and squeaked.

One day she complained, "Clarence, I'm frustrated with this sewing machine. Do you think you could take it apart and clean the parts, then put it back together again? Perhaps it would work better after a cleaning."

Now, young Charles standing nearby heard what his mother said, so he went hunting for a screwdriver and proceeded to take the sewing machine apart without asking either of his parents. As he took out the parts, he laid them in a row in perfect order. Then, he went to Clarence and proudly announced, "Papa, the machine is all apart."

Clarence scratched his head as he observed the parts all over the floor. "Son, you will have to show me how to put it together."

Clarence and Charles tried again and again to put it back together again, but unfortunately, the machine never worked again. Sometime later Clarence surprised Mary with a new treadle Singer sewing machine. Because she loved sewing, Mary squealed in delight when she saw the gift. She continued her sewing for the family, even making men's suits with fine tailoring.

As the Adventist congregations grew in 1909, it became necessary to hold meetings in two halls. Elder Paul Meyer expressed an interest in staying in Lisbon along with his helper, José Abella. So Clarence and Mary decided to move to Villa Nova de Gaia because there were no workers in that city. Since rail travel was limited to that area, the Rentfros sent their furniture and possessions ahead by boat to the area. The family left later by boat, and when they landed, they began looking for a house. For a while they lived at Largo da Bandeira #93 with balconies out over the street and also out in the back. The family enjoyed many pleasant days there. However, they eventually moved into O'Porto where they could reach more people.

They found a four-story house in O'Porto that delighted the whole family at Rua da Boa Vista #145. Located close to the Boa Vista Park and Zoo, the family often enjoyed Sabbath walks there. The house had a winding stairway from the ground floor to the fourth floor. Charles soon learned a quick way to get from the fourth to the first floor on the shiny banister. A large skylight dome on the roof through which the sun shone sent golden rays up and down the winding stairway. A large room on the second floor became the meeting hall for church services. Clarence continued his prolific literature distribution in the area which also included the people in the actual city of O'Porto.

Elder Schwantes built up the work in O'Porto in 1906 and remained until 1909 when he was called back to Brazil. Clarence continued the work there until 1911 when the Rentfros moved again.

> *Clarence mastered the Portuguese language as few Americans have. He spoke the language fluently and wrote it like a well-educated Portuguese man from the University of Coimbra.*

Clarence mastered the Portuguese language as few Americans have. He spoke the language fluently and wrote it like a well-educated Portuguese man from the University of Coimbra. Knowing music aided him in translating many English songs into Portuguese. He taught these songs to his congregations.

One evening, while still living in the four-story house, Clarence reviewed his sermon up-stairs for the evening service. Curtis, the younger son, went to the meeting room, got up behind the pulpit, and announced a song. His sister, Marian, began playing a hymn on the organ. Just then an older man entered the room and seated himself. Curtis looked up and saw the man, so he asked him to say a prayer for the meeting. Reluctant to comply with the little fellow's request, the man said he could not pray. This did not disturb Curtis who then began praying for the old man and exhorting all the people to get ready, for Jesus was coming quickly in the clouds of heaven.

By that time Clarence entered the meeting room and heard the prayer. He stood with bowed head until Curtis finished his prayer. How amazed he felt to see his son become a young preacher although he had not yet entered kindergarten. After the prayer, the old man stood up to leave, and he discovered he was the only one there. Clarence thanked the children for their help and sent them upstairs to bed. Clarence spoke to the man, and that evening he gave his heart to God because of the little sermon and prayer of a child.

One time the Rentfros entertained an elderly Brother Sanchez from Spain who moved to Portugal and lived alone there. Mary prepared a custard for the meal which she often made since she wanted Curtis to gain weight. It was a favorite dish for Curtis. When the dish of custard started to be passed around the table, Curtis looked forward to it coming to his place. However, since Brother Sanchez was the guest, he received the dish first, and Mary told him to help himself. He did so and proceeded to eat all of the custard. Poor Curtis moaned, "There goes my custard!" What a disappointment for Curtis that day. Mary whispered to him that she would make him another one tomorrow.

Mary continued to visit the homes of the sick. Many people kept calling for Missionary Nurse Maria at her home. As a result of Mary's care in one home of five, the family gave their hearts to Christ. The young children who converted to the Adventist message were very eager to become workers for Jesus, and they studied faithfully every day until they were old enough to go out and witness for their Savior. Three of the children became colporteurs and evangelists when grown.

Every day Mary received calls to take care of a sick baby, a mother, or an older child. So many people desired her care, that she had to keep a waiting list. Because she was so busy with nursing, the Rentfros hired a lady to live in to help with the housework and take care of the little children. The long hours of work took their toll on Mary, but she worked on answering every call. Some would come to the Rentfro home knocking on their door in the middle of the night. When Mary heard these nighttime knocks, she often cried, "Clarence, I'm so tired. How can I get up and go out again? Oh, if we only had help to answer all these calls in Portugal!"

"Knock, knock!" the clapper on the door sounded louder. "Senhora, Doña Maria, por favor," a voice called out in the stillness of the night.

Clarence went to the third-floor window and called, "Un momento, senhor." Mary dressed, and Clarence accompanied her on the call. Another night with lost sleep!

Mary did her best to keep up her work with others and her work at home. One time while Mary worked in the kitchen at home, the three Rentfro children played in their backyard by the thick stone wall surrounding the garden. All of a sudden they heard a frantic call from their mother. "Charles, Marian, Curtis. Come to Mama quick."

The three children jumped to their feet in an instant and ran with all their might to their mother who was running out of the house. The instant they ran toward her, the stone wall collapsed because of the trembling of an earthquake that shook the country. When Mary felt the first shaking of the earth, she acted immediately by calling the children and saving them from injury or death. How they all praised the Lord that evening!

*Chapter 41*
# Back Home in Iowa

One day on one of their Sabbath afternoon walks, the family came to a stone wall with a huge iron gate and found the lock snapped tightly shut. Peeking in at the beautiful sights, they saw flowers, marble statues, and a pond with a pair of white swans gliding gracefully among the lovely water lilies. A pleasant gentleman nearby spoke to Clarence and invited him and the family to come inside. They excitedly accepted the invitation, and the lock on the door opened.

They found a beautiful mansion inside the gates that belonged to a very rich man. He guided them through the gardens until they came to an evergreen maze. Proudly he showed them the entrance to the labyrinth and how to follow it to the end. While Clarence stayed to talk with the gentleman and give him literature, Mary and the children tried the labyrinth. The man observed the well-behaved children and later told the family to come again to visit him.

The family spent many pleasant Sabbath afternoons in the lovely gardens while Clarence gave Bible studies to the man. The labyrinth or maze of paths with an eight-foot hedge made it easy to get lost in it. Because the children appeared frightened of getting lost as they wandered through it, Clarence thought of an idea to help. So he took his umbrella, opened it, and raised it high, and then he hurried on ahead through the labyrinth calling the children to look up and follow. As long as the children kept their eyes on the umbrella, they safely made it out at the end of the maze.

One Sabbath afternoon when they arrived at the gate to the mansion and went inside, they found black crepe hanging on the door of the mansion. A gardener met the family there with the sad news that the honorable gentleman recently died. Clarence explained to the children that this ended their visits to the mansion. How sad the family felt about the loss of their friend and the fun they had in the lovely gardens. Because the man had accepted literature and Bible studies, Clarence hoped that he would meet him in heaven.

One day in 1913 Mary received a letter from her mother stating that Susan and her family were coming home on a furlough from China bringing their new Chinese daughter, Oilene. Mother Haskell pleaded with Mary to come home and bring her children from Portugal. She also said, "Since you two girls have been so far away from me, I have had a long time to think over how cruel I was to you in the past." Besides stating her regrets, she said, "I want to love you and your children, too."

Father Haskell and Robert also wanted Mary and her family to come home. After discussing it with Clarence, Mary sent a letter sadly declining the invitation because she found out from Clarence that the Foreign Mission Board lacked money in the treasury to pay for transportation to the United States.

Sometime later Clarence received a letter from the General Conference informing him that he could go ahead and send his family on home now, and he could join them in six months. With that exciting news, a flurry of packing began, and Mary and the three children acquired tickets to travel on the *RMS Anselm* to Liverpool, England, and then to take the *RMS Campania* to New York.

When Mary and the children disembarked from the *RMS Anselm* in England, they had a layover. Feeling uncomfortable with the dock personnel and others hanging around the port, Mary found another lady with her children who felt the same vulnerability. So, they found a room in which they could wait to board the steamship *RMS Campania*. Being fearful of thieves, they barricaded the door with a table, chairs, and a dresser. One man tried to get in, but the women told him to mind his own business. Soon they safely boarded the steamship to New York.

As the ship neared the outer banks of Newfoundland, the passengers received word that they were about to sail over the spot where the Titanic had sunk. The *Campania's* crew threw floral wreaths into the sea, and the orchestra played a somber hymn. This caused Mary and the children to feel fortunate that they were safely on the *Campania*.

## Chapter 41 Back Home in Iowa

After a few more days on the ship, they disembarked and boarded a train to Chicago and then another on to Garwin. What a happy reunion when Father and Robert met them at the station. The children felt excited to take a ride in a buggy. Uncle Rob and Grandpa Haskell sang old hymns to entertain the children as they traveled toward home. Soon they greeted their grandmother who happily welcomed them.

Mary felt sorry that she had missed her sister's visit, but the following day brought many adventures and many Portuguese questions since the children mainly spoke this language. Mary kept busy translating for the children and also for her parents and brother. One day Mother Haskell wanted to take Mary and Marian to visit a neighbor lady on a nearby farm. The ladies began visiting while Marian played in a room with a box full of all sorts of trinkets and toys. All too soon it came time to leave, and the ladies said goodbye.

On the way home Marian seemed noticeably quiet. Evening came, and she remained quiet somewhere in the house. Mary wondered if something was wrong and started searching for Marian. She found her upstairs in their bedroom fascinated with a tiny purse that she opened and shut over and over. Something about the click or snap of opening and shutting it intrigued little Marian.

As Mary entered the room, she asked, "Marian, where did you find that little purse?"

"At the lady's house. She had so many things she didn't need this," answered Marian as she kept clicking the little purse.

Mary pulled Marian up on her lap and told her a story about taking things that did not belong to her. Then, they prayed to Jesus to tell Him how sorry she was for doing that. They decided together that the best thing to do was to return the purse. After that, the purse immediately lost its fascination to Marian. Instead, she seemed eager to get it back to its owner.

The next morning they hitched the horse to the Haskell buggy and drove up the hill to where the lady lived. Surprised to see them at her door, the lady invited them inside, and Mary explained that Marian had something to tell her. Marian gave the lady back the purse and told her in Portuguese how sorry she felt for taking it. She asked for forgiveness with tears running down her cheeks. The lady accepted the purse and the apology with tears in her eyes. She wanted to give Marian the purse, but Marian refused.

Later, when Mary visited Dr. Shunk at the Iowa Sanitarium, she recited the story of the stolen purse to her doctor friend. A few days later,

Marian received a lovely wrapped package. When she opened it, she found a small, beautiful sterling silver purse with a pretty little snap on it and a silver chain handle. Marian felt so proud of her new purse and took it with her wherever she went.

One evening later the Haskell family went to a neighbor's home for a party with many other people. The ladies all placed their coats and purses in the guest bedroom, and Marian had to do the same, much to her displeasure. When it came time to go home and people began gathering their wraps and purses, Marian could not find her precious purse. She cried and cried over the loss even though Mary tried to console her. Now she knew what it was like to have something taken from her. Many years later Mary bought her grown daughter a lovely sterling silver purse as a reminder of her childhood experience in America of stealing and someone stealing from her.

Mary decided to attend the Ames campmeeting because Clarence's sister, Mrs. W. C. Hankins and family, home on furlough from China, were visiting. The Hankins had two adopted daughters, Enid and Beryl, who spoke only Chinese. What a time the cousins had talking Chinese and Portuguese mixed with English! How Mary enjoyed listening!

> *What a time the cousins had talking Chinese and Portuguese mixed with English!*

Mary needed to have a medical treatment at the Iowa Sanitarium, so the grandparents cared for the children while she went to the Sanitarium. Since Mary had enrolled Charles in the Nevada Church School, only the two younger ones stayed at home. So, the grandparents managed everything quite well, and soon Mary returned after her treatment.

Then, one day Clarence arrived from Portugal on his furlough. The children could not stop telling him about the things they saw and the activities they had enjoyed. The family went to see Clarence's mother in Montana and his sister, Bonita, and his brother, Clark. Aunt Bonita gave Marian a beautiful doll, and she received a paint set from another cousin. Later, someone stole the paint set, so Marian had another experience regarding stealing.

At the end of their furlough on May 22, 1913, Clarence attended the General Conference session to report on Portugal, then the family boarded a train to take them to New York and on to England and Portugal. As the family settled on the train, a group of college girls came aboard and presented Marian with a package for her to open on her trip. When she did open the package, she found a beautiful china doll. A sewing class at Washington Missionary College purchased the doll, named her Mildred, and each girl in the class made an outfit for the doll. Each piece of clothing held a label giving the name of the girl who sewed it, and the students decided that the doll should be given to the first missionary family with a little girl leaving the General Conference for a foreign field. This happened to be Marian who gratefully accepted the beautiful doll. It made her feel special and proud to be chosen to receive it. The doll traveled everywhere with her—to Portugal, Brazil, and then back to America. She became a family keepsake.

## Chapter 42

# Back to Portugal

When the family returned to Portugal in June of 1913, Clarence rented a home at Rua St. Helen #12 on the outskirts of O'Porto across the River Douro from where they had previously lived. The family hired a cart man to move their belongings. The bridge across the river required a toll of a charge per wheel. They also inspected the contents of the carts for bottles of wine. As the inspector looked through the family's belongings, he found bottles packed in large boxes. He announced that there would be a charge for each bottle. Clarence told him that his wife canned grape juice, and it was not fermented. The inspector did not believe him, so Clarence unscrewed the cap of one of the bottles and offered the inspector a drink. As the inspector took a sip, a look of surprise crossed his face when he tasted the grape juice. The Rentfros received a permit to cross the bridge without paying a fine, so they finally arrived at their new home and began unpacking.

Another time after the family had settled in, they needed to cross the bridge to visit some Adventist believers on Sabbath. When they set foot on the bridge, the guard came out of his hut and hailed the family to stop. They wondered what could be wrong. Since they were pushing their youngest in the baby carriage, the guard pointed to the four wheels on the carriage and told Clarence he must pay for each wheel. This idea did not please Clarence, so he told Mary to take the baby out of the carriage, and he gave Charles the mattress to carry while Marian carried the blanket.

## Chapter 42  Back to Portugal

Clarence collapsed the carriage, folded it under his arm, and the family marched on across the bridge. The guard gasped in surprise, and he knew he lost his chance to make money on the toll on wheels.

On the weekend afternoons, the Rentfro family took walks to the zoo at the Boa Vista Park or to trails down by the River Douro for enjoyment and to pass out tracts. They learned that the river drained from northern Portugal, flowed through the highland region, and emptied into the Atlantic Ocean near the city of O'Porto. Along the banks of the river, they passed rows and rows of open baskets full of fish. As the sun beat down on this open market and the river breeze circulated the air, the smell of fish became overwhelming, so they often hurried on their way.

One time a boy passed them selling some dry branches of some bush which were used to start fires of coke or charcoal. The open fire was started in a *fogareira* or vessel made of clay fired in a kiln. On this the women placed the cooking utensils, and during the preparation of the meal, the cook must stir with one hand and fan the fire with the other.

Sometimes their walks took them out into the country where they saw women working in the fields cultivating the terraced rice fields. The women wore little black felt hats over colored scarves and tucked their skirts up into their waist sashes so they would not drag in the water. They wore high boots to prevent insects from biting their legs.

At other times as the family walked along the narrow cobbled streets of O'Porto, they saw women sitting on their doorsteps chatting away with neighbors. Some knitted, and others sat and dreamed lazily in the shade of the house. As the Rentfros walked by, they gave the women tracts to read if they were able to read. In the evening peasants walked by going home from the fields, and the fishermen returned vocalizing their sing-song litany of the sea. As the family passed the homes, they smelled fresh sardines grilling for the family supper, which made them walk faster to get away from the oily smell in the air.

On November 21, 1913, the Rentfros' fourth child, Verna May, was born at home. She brought the family so much happiness and became their pride and joy. The family moved to Rua 'd Allianca #127, and a few months later Mary took care of a family with dysentery, causing her to become sick. Then, everyone in the family became sick, even little Verna. Mary took care of the children using all her knowledge of natural remedies and using the loving, gentle touch that only a mother nurse could provide. The older children recovered, but Verna's condition worsened as the days went on. Frightened and frustrated because Verna did not respond,

Mary realized the baby was deteriorating quickly, so she implored Clarence to try to find medical help.

She told him, "If we don't get a doctor, baby Verna won't last the week."

Her words struck terror to the hearts of Clarence and the children. Clarence knew how difficult it would be to find a doctor, but he did his best to find one that would come to treat Verna. He did eventually find one, but by the time the doctor arrived and gave the baby prescribed medicine, it was too late to save her.

Charles woke up about 3:00 a.m., so Mary told him the baby was gone. Charles kissed Verna May's still-warm face as he told her goodbye. When Marian awoke the next morning, which was Sabbath, she heard her parents crying.

She heard her father say, "The Lord gave her to us, and now He has taken her away. Oh, Lord, show us where we failed. Oh, Lord, console us. Shall we call the children and tell them their baby sister is gone?"

Mary answered, "Better wait till daylight." Then, she cried, "Oh, my poor darling baby!" Marian jumped out of bed and ran to her parents' bedroom and clung to her mother, crying as though her heart would break.

That day Mary placed a white tablecloth on a table in the front room and laid the tiny baby gently on a long white pillow all dressed in a pretty bonnet and a long white dress. She looked like a beautiful china doll with her little hands lying gently by her side.

When Curtis saw Verna, he ran to his mother crying, "Mama, cover Baby Sister. She is so cold."

Mary burst into tears. She tried to be so brave for the family, but she broke down in sobs. "Oh, how I will miss my sweet baby girl," she cried.

Clarence made a small white casket. Mary placed a long white pillow in it and around the edge she placed bouquets of violets picked by Marian. Clarence laid the tiny baby in the casket and prepared to conduct the funeral for his little daughter. The O'Porto church members, friends, and neighbors came to support the family, and Clarence preached about the resurrection and the angels who would bring little children back to their mothers' arms.

Everyone accompanied the Rentfros in a funeral procession going to the nearby cemetery called Occidental (now Agramonte) for poor people. Young junior girls carried the casket followed by the family, and everyone else walked behind carrying flowers. Clarence said the final words of farewell at the graveside while most of the people cried.

Curtis started protesting, "Don't put Verna May down into that hole."

## Chapter 42  Back to Portugal

Mary picked him up and cuddled him while whispering comfort to him. Marian began having such pains in her stomach that she doubled over and sobbed. Clarence took her into his arms and explained to her in front of all those attending that Jesus would watch over the baby, and all she had to do was to be a good girl so she could see her again.

Marian cried out loud, "I will be good, Papa."

After that everyone walked away silently down the stony streets and back home. It seemed so lonely at the Rentfro home without their sweet little baby. This loss was very difficult for the family to understand and bear, yet they continued their work for the Lord's sake.

*Chapter 43*
# Sickness and Loss

Time went on with the Rentfros continuing to do whatever they could for the Lord. The groups meeting in several halls kept growing, and the Rentfros kept busy passing out a variety of tracts to interest others. In 1915 they moved to Rua Latino Coelho #265 to reach a new group of people. On December 15 of that year, Clarence Alvin was born. He received much love from his siblings and parents because now their home seemed less lonely. He thrived and enjoyed being the center of so much attention.

One interesting experience the children remember well occurred when they lived there during a miserable winter storm causing huge ocean waves. Because the ocean was so rough, many fishermen could not launch their boats to fish in order to make a living. As the storm persisted, the Rentfros saw something unusual. Charles wrote about it later in life.

"Some of the hungry fishermen walked the weary miles from the coast into Porto. Wearing foul-weather rubberized gear of black hoods and capes, they trudged through the rain-soaked cobbled streets ... they imitated the doleful sounds of wintery gales crying *'Ooh! Ooh! Da-nos pao pelo amor de Deus'* (Give us bread, for the love of God).

"The children felt sad to realize the men and their families did not have food to eat, so they begged Mary for some loaves of bread. Then, from an open window on the upper floor, they tossed the loaves down. How exciting to see the fishermen below catch the loaves in their large black capes. Besides pleasing the children, the fishermen profited from the bread that

## Chapter 43 Sickness and Loss

they could take home to their families."[7] Soon the storm abated, and the fisherman jumped back into their boats and went out to sea.

One day just over a year later Clarence noticed his lymph glands were swollen, so he knew something was wrong. He became very sick with malaria and ran a very high fever. On Sabbath afternoon some of the O'Porto church members came to see him and surrounded his bed. Clarence sat up in bed and announced to them that he was the Pope of Rome. The members acted astonished.

Marian, who followed the visitors into the room, rushed out to hunt Curtis and tell him what their father said. They decided to go tell Charles. When they told him, he reassured them that Papa was not the Pope. He told them that the sickness and the high fever caused their father to say strange things. When the children ran to the bedroom, they found the church members on their knees praying for their sick pastor. Clarence's delirious behavior continued for another day, and he shook and trembled like a tree leaf on a windy day. After about six weeks he recovered.

> *Clarence sat up in bed and announced to them that he was the Pope of Rome.*

Mary also caught malaria and suffered from chills and a high fever. Since she could not nurse little Alvin, he became sick due to the lack of proper food. The older children offered him food, but he wanted his mother's milk. Alvin went into convulsions and became worse day by day. After searching for a Portuguese doctor to examine him, the doctor arrived, but it was too late. Little Alvin died on January 20, 1917, from cerebral meningitis. Another great sadness for the Rentfro family to bear! He was buried in the same cemetery with Verna May. Two sweet babies gone so soon!

The day after the funeral Clarence received word from the General Conference inviting the family to move to Brazil in South America where he would become superintendent of the school there. They accepted, and as they began preparations to move, the family felt less gloomy and sad as they thought about the adventure of going to another foreign land as missionaries. After packing, they procured passports and tickets for the steamship *S.S.Champlain* in February of 1917.

However, the ship never reached port because it was sunk by the Germans as it headed toward Portugal. World War I raged on in Europe. Then, they received notice that the war transport *S.S. Admiral Rigoult de Genouilly*,

---
7   Rentfro, C.A. *The House of Bread*. Perspective Digest, No. 3, p. 42-46, 1996.

a freighter without accommodations, would take on passengers on March 17. The ship was on its way to Argentina to pick up a load of horses for Africa and would stop in Brazil, so they purchased tickets for this ship.

Before they left, the children asked their parents to take them once more to the cemetery where their little siblings rested. They walked to the cemetery and stood beside the little graves of Verna May and Clarence Alvin. Clarence told the children again about the resurrection, and with tears in their eyes, the little family bowed their heads while each prayed and promised to be true and faithful so they could meet the little ones on resurrection morning. They left the cemetery with sorrowful hearts for they knew they would never see the graves again.

At that time Clarence paid $20.00 for the upkeep for the graves. He thought surely that the Lord would come before the money was used up. However, time passed, and the money eventually was gone, and the cemetery officials placed other bodies in the places where the babies were buried. So, now, no one can find their graves, but Jesus has them marked, and when He comes again He will place the sweet babies in Mary's arms.

With only ten days left before they sailed, final preparations rushed on. Clarence preached his farewell sermon the very next Sabbath exhorting the O'Porto members to be faithful and carry on the work of the Lord in that city. Elder Paul Meyer from the Lisbon church would watch over all the congregations now.

The Rentfros sent their possessions by cart hauled by a donkey to the dock, so that they could be ready for loading on the ship. When the day came for them to leave, the family walked to the streetcar stop and took their last ride from Rua Latina Coelho to the Port of Leixoes. The church members accompanied them to the dock to see the family off on their trip because, as a farewell gift, Clarence paid the streetcar fare for each one to go with them.

The church group stood around the Rentfro family singing a farewell song and then bowing their heads in a farewell prayer. Clarence prayed for the work in Portugal, for the members to be true and faithful, and asked that God would send guardian angels to protect them on their trip to Brazil. A dangerous trip lay ahead because of the fighting of World War I. The family boarded the launch to take them out to the ship, and as the small boat pulled away from the dock, the Adventist group on shore began waving their handkerchiefs in farewell. Many tears flowed from the group and also from the family. After thirteen years of living and working in Portugal, they all felt as close as a family, and everyone felt sad to say goodbye.

## Chapter 43  Sickness and Loss

So, on March 17, 1917, the launch made its way close to the *SS Admiral Renault de Genolier*, a French freighter. The sailors came down the gangplank to help the family aboard. The children felt excited to be sailing on a big ship again.

*Chapter 44*
# Sailing on a Freighter

"What kind of boat is this?" one of the children asked the parents. When the parents told them it was a freighter, the children wanted to see where they were going to stay. The steward ushered them down a flight of stairs to the lower part of the ship to a stateroom that would be their home while on board. The steward instructed them to cover the portholes at night so no light would shine through to the enemy lurking about in submarines.

As they entered the designated "stateroom" area, mouths flew open. The Rentfros looked around in amazement. Clarence remarked, "There must be some mistake." He shook his head for he saw stalls instead of rooms.

"What are they used for?" Charles asked.

"For horses," the steward replied.

"For horses?" the children repeated in unison.

Finally gaining his composure, Clarence asked as he pointed to the far end of the long row, "May we have that corner?"

Any place seemed agreeable to the steward. So, Mary and Clarence began to arrange the corner to look like a stateroom. There were no comfortable beds with clean sheets, blankets, or bedspreads. No stewardess came to help the passengers get settled.

Although the parents were still rather shocked, the children became excited about the idea of having two portholes to look out at the water

## Chapter 44  Sailing on a Freighter

and sky during the day. Curtis thought maybe they would see fish darting around or seagulls flying low to catch the fish.

"Maybe a ship or a submarine might pass by," he dreamed.

Clarence saw some canvas piled up in the middle of the ship, so he asked the steward for enough canvas to curtain off their section. He began hanging the canvas from hooks on the ceiling and around the long pipes to separate the horse stalls. Each stall had a long manger four feet from the floor. Clarence placed a wood platform on top of each of them and secured it tightly to the mangers. They found mattresses to place on the platforms, and Mary unpacked their bedrolls which contained the sheets, pillows, and blankets. Soon the sleeping quarters were all arranged. They stacked the suitcases neatly in a corner and set up a washstand in a convenient spot. For a clothes closet, Clarence strung a rope across one end of the side on the canvas wall.

This is how a missionary family roughing it on a freighter made a fairly comfortable living area for themselves. This new "home" excited the children, and they began asking about what other exciting adventures might occur.

"We will see," said Mary as she gathered them together for some motherly advice. "When the ship sails, you must stay close and obey me."

She also gave them much instruction on how to behave themselves on board the ship. There would be much to see and do, but some time must be spent in the stateroom reading, studying, and resting. Cautioning the children about not going too close to the railing of the freighter, she explained how they could be rolled over into the ocean and swept away by the dashing waves on a rough day at sea. She told them she would be busy cooking the family meals in the kitchen since she obtained permission from the captain to do so.

"But, where will we eat?" asked Charles.

"Well, on nice days we'll eat out on the open deck."

With that Clarence took all the children up to the deck to look for a safe, convenient place to eat. They saw large ropes called "howser lines" coiled up in a corner of the deck and placed in a circle. The circle seemed large enough to accommodate the family, and it looked like a safe area.

"Let's ask if we can have that space," suggested Charles. Clarence found the steward and obtained permission to use the rope area as their permanent spot to eat. The children thought it would be fun to sit inside the ropes. When the freighter rocked from side to side, they would be held safely by the large coiled-up ropes.

Since Charles was the eldest, he was their explorer. He wanted to find out all he could from the French marines who were in charge of the large naval guns over the stern of the freighter.

"What are they for?" the younger children asked their brother.

"The ship needs those guns for protection from the Germans," he informed them.

"Will we see a German submarine?" Curtis questioned.

"We hope not," Charles answered. "We have asked the Lord for protection, and He will take care of His children. Don't be afraid, Curtis and Marian," Charles explained to the younger children in a tender and reassuring manner.

Soon the freighter was all loaded, so the marines raised the anchor and the smokestacks began puffing out dark smoke. The ship started moving, so the family went out on the deck to take a last look at the land they called home for so many years, and the only home the children knew. As they moved farther out to sea, their home port faded in the distance.

"I think I still see a white handkerchief," Mary told her husband. "My heart already aches for those poor faithful souls who loved us and depended on our care all these years."

Tears filled Clarence's eyes as he gazed back over the blue waters toward the O'Porto shore. He said goodbye in his heart, for he could no longer see nor hear his Portuguese friends.

During the trip their ship's activities followed a routine. The first day they spent getting acquainted with the seamen. Charles followed some of them around as he watched the rugged work they performed. However, the guns intrigued him the most. He also kept watch for submarines to appear in the water by looking for an enemy periscope to pop up out of the ocean. The seamen told him that the periscope was the dangerous part of the submarine.

Once in a while, the ship moved away from black floating objects bobbing up and down in the ocean. Could they be foreign mines? Perhaps the best thing to do would be to move cautiously away from them, which the ship did. After several days and nights of quiet sailing over smooth waters, the freighter slowly approached the Lisbon harbor, their first stop.

Mary arose early to go to the kitchen to prepare breakfast. In the kitchen she became acquainted with the Portuguese, Spanish, Chinese, and French cooks busily working on the daily meals. In huge black kettles, they placed meat, vegetables, onions, and other items. However, Mary fixed very simple meals for the family each day without meat. As they

## Chapter 44  Sailing on a Freighter     189

gathered to eat in their chosen rope corner, the sea breeze would add salty spray to their meals.

Later in the day, the freighter glided in toward the Lisbon harbor as the Rentfros stood on deck gazing toward the land. They saw familiar sights again—shoreline, boats, nets, fishermen putting out to sea, and the women left behind. The faces of the men looked weather-beaten by the winds of the sea and the burning sun. Because they lived with so little of this world's goods and because they had so little hope, it put a burden on the hearts of Clarence and Mary. Now they left it all in the hands of Elder Paul Meyer from the Latin Union Conference.

The ship dropped anchor, and the launch came out to pick up the passengers who wanted to go to shore. The Rentfro family rode the launch to land and went to see Elder Meyer. They stayed the night and had a good visit together knowing that they would likely never see each other again. It was reported later that Paul Meyer died in Auschwitz in 1944.

On the way back to the launch they stopped at the market and bought food supplies to take on board. The members of the Lisbon church came to say goodbye bringing goodies to the family including a box of figs. Then the family lined up to board the launch, showed their tickets and passports, and soon were off to the ship.

When they reached the large freighter, the family took their turn climbing the rope ladder and accepting the help of the friendly sailors to get on deck. A sailor called a pursuer checked the passengers in, so they waited. Just then Mary saw six young men go past the pursuer as he began checking the tickets and passport of their family. A cook dressed in white standing nearby motioned to the men to go on to the quarters below. The six young men disappeared.

Soon the freighter pulled up anchor after all the cargo was loaded. Once again the Rentfro family waved goodbye to the first fruits of their early labors for the Lord in Lisbon. They saw Elder and Mrs. Paul Myer, Mrs. Portugal, the Figueredos, and others that came to say goodbye to the pastor and his family who were the very first Seventh-day Adventist pioneers in Portugal. Again the white handkerchiefs waved goodbyes both on shore and from the Rentfros on the ship.

Soon the freighter began plugging along through the blue ocean waves on to its next destination, Dakar, Africa, nine days away. Smooth sailing with no storms in sight helped all the passengers to enjoy the trip. New passengers set up their own staterooms with canvas curtains. The Rentfro children found new friends among the newcomers and spent many happy hours playing with them.

*Chapter 45*

# On to Africa and Beyond

To break the monotony of the slow sailing, a frisky, black and white fox terrier belonging to one of the ship's officers grabbed a shoe from a young lady passenger and tossed it over the railing. Both the officer and the young lady looked shocked. The dog kept bouncing around them, and soon several people broke out in laughter at the incident.

> *A frisky, black and white fox terrier belonging to one of the ship's officers grabbed a shoe from a young lady passenger and tossed it over the railing.*

During mealtime each party took its turn in the line at the kitchen door to receive a meal, and often an extra man showed up. Clarence noticed one young stowaway and began getting acquainted with him. He gave the young man a Bible and studied with him every day.

When Sabbath arrived, Clarence conducted Sabbath School and church in their stateroom. The passengers noticed this and asked questions. This gave Clarence the opportunity to witness about the truths he loved.

The days passed and another shore loomed in the distance. The Rentfros and the other passengers wondered what they would see in Africa.

## Chapter 45  On to Africa and Beyond     191

Then, out of the fog, came a pilot ship to meet the freighter. After the gangplank was lowered, a group of African sailors came aboard. They ordered the passengers to line up, and then they went to the quarters to search among the partitioned stalls. They finally found the six young men hiding behind the luggage. They handcuffed them and took them into custody.

The passengers looked in amazement to see the six young men marched off the freighter. It seemed that they were trying to escape to South America. Lisbon had sent word to Dakar to search the freighter for these deserters from the war. As the men left the ship, a passenger slipped his passport into the last man's hip pocket. The head soldier asked Clarence to come to police headquarters to translate from Portuguese into French for the police. The children and Mary waited on board for Clarence to return.

After the men were taken into custody, the passengers were allowed to disembark, and cargo was unloaded. Mary went to the kitchen to get dinner so the meal would be ready when Clarence returned. The passengers got in line to receive their food, and then they sat on the floor of the deck eating while the Rentfro family settled inside the coiled ropes to eat.

Suddenly two tall black men dressed in flowing white robes with headgear appeared on board looking at each of the passengers. As they stepped among the groups on the deck floor eating, one of the ladies offered the men each a plate of food. The men graciously accepted the plates. They smelled the food and began discussing it in a foreign language. Each man shook his head and gave a disgusted look. Then, they quickly threw the plates with the food over the rail into the waters below. The women looked surprised and became angry at the ingratitude of the men.

The two black men moved over to the Rentfro group inside the ropes. Looking at the food on the plates of Mary and the children, they acted interested in it. Mary figured out that they wanted a plate of their food. She thought about it and decided to let them try her cooking. She placed some of the simple food on two plates and handed it to the men along with a fork. They took the plates and moved over to the railing. A Portuguese lady called to Mary, "Your plates will be thrown into the ocean, too. Just wait and see."

When the men tasted Mary's food, a smile came over their faces. They finished the food and handed the plates back to Mary. They bowed politely and happily waved goodbye. Jealousy overcame one of the Portuguese ladies because the men threw away the good meat and other items on her plates. This incident gave Mary the opportunity to witness for the

Lord and explain the difference between a meat and a vegetarian meal. She learned later that the Dakar people were Mohammedans (currently referred to as Muslims) and did not eat pork.[8]

Soon Clarence returned bringing with him the young man to whom he gave the Bible. The children felt happy that this man escaped punishment by the Portuguese government.

A few of the African people came on board also to look around. The steward warned the passengers to watch their personal belongings. Nothing unusual happened until later in the evening when it was time for supper. The Rentfro family sat inside their rope coils eating when suddenly a shower of peanuts in their shells came pouring into Mary's lap and around the children. Looking up in surprise they saw a young black Mohammedan boy standing there grinning so sweetly at the American family. He kept unloading peanuts from his flowing robe pockets to the amazement of everyone.

"Oh, how wonderful! Thank you so much," Mary spoke gratefully to the boy. The peanuts would last a long time and were a good source of protein. She gave the boy a loaf of freshly baked bread from the kitchen. With the loaf under his arm, he bowed low and graciously waved goodbye. As he left to descend the gangplank, the three Rentfro children watched him from the railing. He kept glancing back and waving at the children as he walked away. When he reached the end of the dock, he stopped a moment and waved a final farewell as he disappeared out of sight. Mary believed his gift came from his father, who had eaten and enjoyed Mary's food earlier.

The Portuguese lady whose food went over the railing acted sad because she did not receive a peanut shower. Mary, always generous and kind, gave the lady some of her peanuts. In her heart Mary hoped the lady learned that a vegetarian diet is superior to meat diets.

Since the freighter would be in port another day, Clarence promised the children they would all explore Dakar tomorrow. The children had difficulty sleeping that night thinking about the exciting things to see the next day. They kept peeking out of the portholes watching the scenes below till Papa said they must go to sleep.

Clarence woke the family the next day saying, "Let's get an early start to see the sights of Dakar while they're still loading cargo."

After a hearty breakfast, they descended the gangplank and passed Dakar's inspection. The family walked briskly past the dock officials, army officials, soldiers and people clothed in flowing white robes with their heads covered in turbans. Women appeared dressed in colorful gowns with flowers in their noses.

---

8   http://1ref.us/r9. Accessed 12/10/18

## Chapter 45  On to Africa and Beyond

After passing the warehouses along the harbor, they came into full view of an open-air market. Black men, women, and children shouted about their wares for sale which were lined up in baskets side by side. People were milling around looking at the goodies of the land.

The family walked on and found a lovely park with plenty of room for children to run and play. After being on board ship with no place for running, the children burst with energy and exercised their legs for quite a while.

Then Clarence wanted to see how people lived away from the city, so he hired a black Mohammedan with a horse-drawn carriage for the day. The family saw groups of naked men, women, and children milling about in a carefree manner with not much to bother them or to occupy their time and minds. Children scampered here and there in the dust with dogs or pigs. The sightseers traveled on till they came to a small village out in the desert with similar scenes, so since the sun began creeping down the sky, they motioned to the driver to turn around so they could go back to the ship. The driver shook his head No as he stood by his horse and motioned with his hands that the harness broke, and he could not fix it. If Clarence would give him some money, he could get someone to fix it. Now Clarence realized the driver might be up to something, so he walked up to the horse, looked it over, and tightened a loosened buckle. But the driver would not budge. Not to be outdone, Clarence hopped into the driver's seat, picked up the reins and started off. The startled driver yelled for him to stop. Clarence called back, "Come with me if you want to get back to town."

The driver came running, so Clarence let him take the reins back. The driver acted upset for a while, but when Clarence started talking to him in French, he brightened up. He understood that these passengers were too clever for him.

The family arrived safely back at the open-air market and purchased some carrots, cabbage, celery, nuts, bread, and other supplies for the rest of the trip to South America. They made it back to the ship in time, and the sailors were happy to see them again.

After the long day's outing, the children showed signs of weariness, so off to bed they went, happy that they saw a small part of Africa on a day they would long remember.

*Chapter 46*
# The End of the Journey

Several days later word spread throughout the crew and passengers to get ready for a health inspection. The ship's doctor got ready to vaccinate all on board due to the spread of smallpox. The Rentfros lined up with the others near the doctor's compartment. As the line moved along, Mary noticed to her horror that all the passengers got their vaccination with the same lance which the doctor disinfected with a flame from the kerosene lamp. However, they all received the vaccination, which took effect as their fevers rose and arms swelled. Soon they all recovered.

On one occasion the gunner who guarded the guns observed an unusual object in the ocean. A whistle alerted the crew and passengers for an attack by the enemy. Avoiding the object, the ship traveled slowly onward. There were fewer mines now that the ship plowed farther south, since the war centered mostly near the coasts of England and Europe. Every day in the Rentfros' family worship they asked the Lord for His protection from any enemy lurking in the ocean. How thankful they were for a safe journey.

One day they heard that land was sighted because the ship was nearing South America. They could see mountains way in the distance. In order to try to see the land, Clarence and the children went to the prow of the ship. They noticed three pilot fish guiding the ship as they leaped up in the air and over the waves. They kept this up for several days as the ship plugged away toward land. Sometimes the fish swam away, then they came back

## Chapter 46  The End of the Journey

again and took their positions. Clarence pointed out to the children that this was like God's constant care over them.

Another day the captain posted an alert because of an enemy submarine's periscope or a mine people thought they saw. The ship stopped for five hours to check things out. The Rentfro family continued to ask the Lord for His protection from the enemy and thanked Him for the safe journey so far.

After several days the passengers lined up along the railing to look at the fascinating sights of a South American port called Recife. They saw English warships, sailboats, and fishing vessels near the port. A launch came alongside to pick up the mail. No one went ashore at this port.

After a few more days the freighter dropped anchor at the Port of Bahia where the passengers were allowed to disembark. The young man whom Clarence befriended told the Rentfros he wanted to go ashore to see relatives. The children jumped around eager to get off the ship and feel ground beneath their feet again. So all the Rentfros got off the ship to see Bahia, and they were excited to hear people speaking Portuguese. As they walked around the streets, they saw familiar sights, such as men emptying their fishing nets into baskets and ladies carrying baskets of fish, fruit, and other wares on their heads. This all made the Rentfros feel at home, and they decided they would like living in Brazil.

Soon it was time to return to the ship. When they reached the port, they noticed the young man Clarence had befriended had not returned like the other passengers. Marian told her parents that she remembered seeing him walk slowly away at first looking at this and that. Then suddenly he increased his pace and faded out of sight.

So, the family boarded the launch, then ascended the rope ladder to the freighter. When Marian climbed up, a sailor took her under her arms to lift her to the deck. She let out a sharp cry of pain because the lymph gland under her arm was still swollen from the vaccination. Her scream frightened the sailor, and he dropped Marian. However, he instantly grabbed her around her waist before she hit the water below. What a narrow escape for Marian!

> *Her scream frightened the sailor, and he dropped Marian. However, he instantly grabbed her around her waist before she hit the water below.*

Clarence brought a whole bunch of bananas back with him. Soon Mary prepared a delicious meal of oranges, bananas, mangoes, nuts, and Brazilan long, hard, white rolls. It all tasted so good.

At sea again, and after a few more days passed, they saw land again. This is where they would disembark and stay, for it was the place they expected to live. They saw the mountains on the horizon as well as fishing boats and junk rafts carrying the fishermen out to sea.

"Look, Marian," Curtis called to his sister. "See that fisherman in the *jungarda* with lots of fish."

"We'll like this country, Curtis," said Marian. "It's like our Portugal that we left. Look at all those fishermen going out to sea and coming back again with all that fish."

The children talked back and forth in Portuguese, the language they loved. They knew some words of English but not enough to carry on a conversation.

Soon the ship blasted its foghorn announcing to others that it was coming into port and to call the pilot ship to come and guide it into the harbor. A pilot ship showed up, and soon the freighter stopped its engines and dropped anchor. The harbor pilot and health officials came aboard to inspect the ship, the crew, and the passengers. After giving a clean bill of health to all aboard, the inspectors left and went back to the pilot ship, which guided the freighter into the harbor of Rio de Janiero.

The children could hardly wait to get on land again. They had lived on the freighter from March 17 to April 8, 1917. Charles went up to the front of the ship to see the new land clearly. Curtis and Marian stayed with their parents looking over the ship's railing. How grateful to God they all felt to be landing in their new home at last.

**The End**

# *Epilogue*

The information for this story of Mary ends with the family getting ready to disembark in Brazil because the eleven handwritten notebooks by their daughter, Marian, end there. There is a possibility that more handwritten notebooks exist, but they could not be located.

I was able to glean some additional information about Mary and her family from a book on Portugal's centennial, 1904–2004. The report is that when they left Portugal, two Seventh-day Adventist churches existed with a total of about 100 members.

In Brazil, Clarence assumed the presidency of Mission Mineira. When they arrived in Rio de Janeiro on April 8, 1917, they were met by two members referred to as brothers Kumpel and Ehlers who helped them get settled. The three children directly came down with the measles and had to be cared for in members' homes, since the Rentfros had no residence at the time.

While the children recovered, their nurse mother stayed by their sides, and Clarence visited the companies and churches in the area. He also spent time studying Portuguese as spoken in Brazil, which seemed necessary since some reported that they could not understand his Portugal Portuguese.

After that he did some evangelism in Rio de Janeiro for two months and then transferred to the state of Minas to work and to establish a home for Mary and the children. While there, he was busy constantly traveling and performing many baptisms as a result of the work of colporteurs and lay members. In 1917 in Brazil he baptized more believers than during his thirteen years in Portugal.

Mary taught school to her children and then developed a medical missionary work in Juiz de Fora by visiting the sick and administering treatments. She treated many patients with bronchitis and intestinal disturbances. One report tells how she, accompanied by J. E. Brown, found a very ill five-year-old boy. She dedicated her time and skill to him until he became well. Because of this, she received the sympathy of the family and increased their interest in the church.

Clarence did some writing for the periodicals in Brazil and wrote an article called "Health Work in Brazil," which appeared in the *Adventist Review* (unable to document if it was the English version or Portuguese version). In the article he lauded Mary's previous experience as a health worker among the sick in Portugal. He also said she cooperated with doctors and did not charge unless the family could afford to pay a small amount. He stated that she had all the work she could handle. Begging for nurses to come to Brazil to teach health principles and the gospel to the poor people there, he also told of the need for clinics to be established there.

Some reports say that Mary handled thirty-five baby deliveries within the two years they served in that area along with all her other nursing calls. During the flu epidemic a large number of people died, but Mary, with God's help, saved the lives of many patients and instructed them in correct daily living.

In 1922 Clarence became president of the Pernambucan Mission, which was located north of the Rio Grande River. The mosquito population thrived in that area. It was at this location that his malaria surfaced again with two attacks in one month.

So, in 1923, he transferred to the Brazil Adventist College in Sao Paulo where he taught Bible and history. Mary taught nursing practices and childcare. It also gave the children the opportunity to attend good schools in that location.

However, for reasons of health that were not described, the Rentfros left the mission field in July of 1924 at Sao Paulo on the *RMS Voltaire* heading to New York City. After their return to the United States, Clarence pastored in North Dakota, Wisconsin, and Michigan until 1938, when he and Mary retired to Baldwin Park, a small town in California where their son, Curtis, and his wife, Mildred, had purchased a home after their son, George, was born. Mary and Clarence lived for some time in a small cottage on the property owned by Curtis.

Mary and Clarence persuaded Marian's family to move there to teach in the local Adventist elementary school. They did so, and then Mary and Clarence bought a home next door to Marian and her family. Several of the grandchildren grew up there. They had many pleasant memories of Clarence and Mary. One remembered they had a family pet named Polly the Parrot who lived in an iron cage in their house.

When Marian's husband, DeGrove, opened his medical office, he employed Curtis' wife as the office nurse. Mary took the exam to become a registered nurse at the age of sixty-one and passed, so she also worked there for several decades. DeGrove employed Curtis as the x-ray technician and lab assistant, Charles as office manager and purchasing agent, and Marian as the billing clerk. Curtis' daughter, Barbara, often ran errands for them.

Clarence died in 1951 at 74 years of age in a hospital in Covina, California, due to injuries caused by an accident. All of his family attended the funeral, and he was buried in a memorial park near Loma Linda University where he was eventually joined by Mary and Marian's family. Marian's husband, DeGrove, who admired and respected Mary, took loving care of her for the rest of her life. Several times he, and occasionally Curtis, took her and other family members to Iowa to visit the Haskell family and to visit Mary's sister, Susan Wilbur, and her family in Oregon. Mary passed away on April 26, 1972, at the age of 97.

**Charles**, the oldest son, became a professor of business at Brazil Adventist College and served as treasurer and business manager until 1935. At first the school was a secondary school with only the first year of college available there. The enrollment at that time was 100. In 1936 he moved to Washington, D.C., to work as statistical secretary at the General Conference. He married Esther Allen, born on October 4, 1908, in Takoma Park, Maryland, and on their 50th wedding anniversary they traveled to Portugal to revisit places from his childhood. He wrote about his visit in the *Adventist Review* of September 11, 1980 (pp. 18, 19). Esther passed away on June 3, 1986, and Charles married Sylvia Buckman, the widow of Pastor Watson Buckman, in 1988. They visited Madeira and Lisbon on their honeymoon. Charles died on June 22, 1999, in Grand Junction, Colorado.

Charles' older daughter, Arloene, was born in Maternity Hospital in Sao Paulo in 1930. She has a BS in Nursing and holds an MPH from Loma Linda University. She became a nurse educator and worked in Colorado. On June 24, 1951, she married John Goley, a pastor who graduated from Union College with a degree in theology plus earning a master's degree in church history at the Seminary in Washington, D.C., on June 24, 1951. After teaching school for four years, John pastored in Kansas, Colorado, and New Mexico. He and Arloene are now retired in Grand Junction, Colorado.

They had three children—John, born on February 3, 1954, Michael, and Brenda. John graduated with a PhD in health education from Loma Linda University. He married Kathy Sheideman, who is a church school teacher. Second son, Michael, was stillborn on August 30, 1956. Daughter Brenda was born in Wichita, Kansas, on September 2, 1963.

She is an RN and has a BS in nursing from Union College. She married Randall Morris on December 22, 1984, who graduated from Union College with a BA in accounting and is currently self-employed. They have four children who have canvassed—Esther, Titus, Levi, and Gracie, age 14, who canvassed the summer of 2018.

Charles' younger daughter, Elaine, was born December 10, 1931, in Sao Paulo, Brazil, and married Roderick Davis in San Fernando, California. They have two children—Gregory, born in Bellingham, Washington, who is currently a bank loan officer, and Kurt, born in Atascadero, California, who is a health consultant, and was married June 14, 1981, to Evie Brown, a school teacher. They have three children—Matt, Hannah, and Will.

The only surviving daughter of Clarence and Mary, **Marian**, attended Cheyenne River Academy at Harvey, North Dakota, and Emmanuel Missionary College Academy at Berrien Springs, Michigan. She graduated from Western State Teachers College in June 4, 1935. On June 11 of the same year, she married William DeGrove Padgett.

Following her marriage she taught with her husband in SDA church schools in Bedford and Pontiac in Michigan before moving to California in 1939. In California the family moved to Baldwin Park where her parents lived, and she taught at the SDA church schools in Baldwin Park besides schools in Redlands and in Los Angeles at the Lincoln Park School.

DeGrove decided to go into the medical field, so he entered the College of Medical Evangelists (now called Loma Linda University), and graduated in September, 1945. Eventually he purchased the medical practice in Baldwin Park and employed several family members. Later he became an anesthesiologist and taught student nurses. After some failed pregnancies, the couple privately adopted two boys named Allen and Dwayne, born to two separate single mothers who were patients of DeGrove.

Marian continued to teach church school for years, then taught piano until her death. Allen was born one year after Dwayne on October 8, 1947.

Allen graduated from San Gabriel Academy and died of cancer in 1970 at age 23 while studying dentistry in his second year of Dental School at Loma Linda University. Dwayne was born on October 8, 1946. He graduated from San Gabriel Academy, and after junior college he graduated from Cal Poly Pomona College of Engineering. He began graduate study, but when his brother, Allen, died, he left school. He married Wendy Potter on January 14, 1984. She has a PhD in physics and teaches in that area. They have two daughters, Corrie and Carrie, who are married and live in California. Dwayne retired as an engineer at the Jet Propulsion Lab in Pasadena, California.

The younger son of Clarence and Mary, **Curtis**, attended and graduated from Iron River Academy and went on to Andrews University in Michigan. He moved to California and attended Glendale Sanitarium and Hospital Nursing School and after graduation became a registered nurse in 1934. He married a classmate, Mildred Parmley, on December 24, 1934, who also became a registered nurse. They had two children, George Alvin and Barbara Jean.

George married Kathryn Agnes Price on March 9, 1962. He graduated from college in 1962 and worked in sales until he began a career as a tile and marble building contractor. They have three sons—Kurtis, Kristopher, and Ryan—who each are building contractors and excel in the tile and marble business. Their daughter, Kwynn, is a building sales representative. Ryan graduated from California State University in San Bernardino, then went on to receive a master's degree in business administration from the University of Redlands.

Mary, as a midwife, assisted in the birth of Barbara Jean who later in life met Richard Post at Pacific Union College. They were married on September 4, 1960. Barbara became a registered nurse and worked as a director of nurses and as RN consultant in the long-term and post-acute industry for many years. Barbara's husband, Richard, after graduating from California State University in San Francisco, went on to graduate school and went into business. He retired as Director of Western Sales for a national corporation in Chicago, Illinois. They have three daughters, Jennifer, Alison, and Melissa who attended college where Jennifer majored in English; Alison in early childhood education, and Melissa, after graduating from Loma Linda University, became a registered nurse. She is said to look the most like her great-grandmother, Mary. The three girls have taken mission trips to Central America and Mexico. Melissa was a missionary in Guyana, South America, for ten years.

Curtis loved studying and took classes all his life. He became an x-ray technician and medical technologist and then took classes in pre-law because he seriously considered becoming an attorney. He and his wife moved to Orange, California, in 1965 where he worked in a cardiac cauterization lab which utilized all the medical skills he had acquired over the years. He passed away February 24 at age fifty-five of a heart attack. Some thought that because of his premature birth, he might have had a leaky heart valve.

It is interesting to note that quite a few of Mary's descendants have entered the medical field, some have been missionaries, and some have also canvassed. What joy she will experience in heaven when she reunites with her large and dedicated family members!

We have some information on Mary's brothers, Robert and Marshall. Marshall was born on April 2, 1871, in Tama County, Iowa. He married Mary Ella Hayes, and they had seven children. He died March 8, 1944, at age 73. Robert was born July 15, 1876, and married Minerva Caroline Stull. They had four children. He was a farmer all his life and died January 21, 1970. Some of their descendants are Seventh-day Adventists.

Mary's sister, Susan, was born December 18, 1872, and died July 31, 1965, in Portland, Oregon. As it states in this book, she married Edwin Wilbur on July 21,1902, and they spent several years in China as medical missionaries. They were among the first missionaries to enter China and spent time in Hong Kong and Canton, and where Edwin died of malaria. Susan and Edwin had two birth sons, Robert and Frederick, plus an adopted Chinese girl named Oilene. Several of Susan's descendants have served in the educational and medical fields within the denomination and in other areas.

The friendly Adventist neighbor, known only as Mrs. Payne, who invited the Haskell children to church, will be shocked when she arrives in heaven and sees the amazing result of her kindness in the number of Susan and Mary's descendants who have served the church and humanity.

# *Mary's Egg Spread*

Boil and mash several eggs

Chop one stalk of celery

Dash of salt

Mix with enough olive oil to make a spread

Slice a loaf of French bread in half lengthwise

Spread with above ingredients

Note: This recipe is perhaps the one Mary used to prevent her family from dying of starvation.

# Bibliography

Inter-European Division News & *Adventist Review. President of Portugal Visits Adventist Church in Lisbon* (March 5, 2018). http://1ref.us/r6 (accessed December 6, 2018)

"Billy Sunday" Wikipedia. Accessed 12/10/183. "Boc de Inferno." Wikipedia. http://1ref.us/r8. Accessed 12/10/18.

Rentfro, Clarence K. "Worldwide Field—Portugal." *Advent Review and Sabbath Herald.* July 23, 1908. p. 12.

Rentfro, C.A. "The House of Bread." *Perspective Digest*, No. 3, p. 42–46, 1996.

"Mohammedanism." Wiktionary. http://1ref.us/r9. Accessed 12/10/18.

# For Further Reading

"Portuguese Explorers." Elizabethan-era.org. http://1ref.us/rb. Accessed 12/20/18.

Ferreira, Ernesto. *Arautos de Boas Novas*, Uniao Portuguesa dos Adventistas do Setimo Dia, 2008.

"Billy Sunday." *Christianity Today.* http://1ref.us/rc. Accessed 12/20/18.

Olsen, M. Ellsworth. *Origin and Progress of Seventh-day Adventists.* Washington, D.C.: Review and Herald Publishing Association, 1926.

Schwarz, R. W. & Greenleaf, F. *Light Bearers*. Nampa, ID: Pacific Press Publishing Association, 1995.

E. Spalding, A. W. *Origin and History of Seventh-day Adventists*, Vol. 2., pp.79–90. Washington D.C.: Review and Herald Publishing Association, 1962.

Office of Adventist Archives, Statistics, and Research. http://1ref.us/rd. Accessed 12/20/18.

Spalding, A.W. *Captains of the Host*. Washington, D.C.: The Review and Herald Publishing Association, 1949. http://1ref.us/re. Accessed 12/20/18.

Spalding, A.W. *Christ's Last Legion*. Washington, D.C.: The Review and Herald Publishing Association, 1949. http://1ref.us/rf. Accessed 12/20/18.

Spalding, A.W. *Footprints of the Pioneers*. Washington, D.C.: The Review and Herald Publishing Association, 1947. http://1ref.us/rg. Accessed 12/20/18.

Dick, E. PhD, *Founders of the Message*. Washington, D.C.: The Review and Herald Publishing Association, 1938. http://1ref.us/rh. Accessed 12/20/18.

Schwarz, R.W. *Light Bearers to the Remnant*. Mountain View, CA: Pacific Press Publishing Association, 1979.

## TEACH Services, Inc.
PUBLISHING

We invite you to view the complete
selection of titles we publish at:
**www.TEACHServices.com**

We encourage you to write us
with your thoughts about this,
or any other book we publish at:
**info@TEACHServices.com**

TEACH Services' titles may be purchased in
bulk quantities for educational, fund-raising,
business, or promotional use.
**bulksales@TEACHServices.com**

Finally, if you are interested in seeing
your own book in print, please contact us at:
**publishing@TEACHServices.com**

We are happy to review your manuscript at no charge.

www.ingramcontent.com/pod-product-compliance
Lightning Source LLC
Chambersburg PA
CBHW070551160426
43199CB00014B/2458